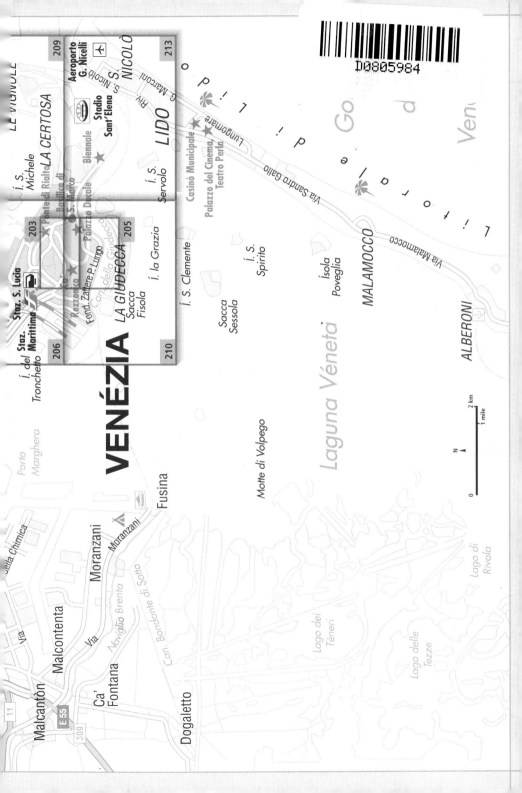

Venice is a sheer delight. The city's unique architecture, its network of canals, and the play of light over the lagoon entrances every visitor: the view from the Riva degli Schiavoni over the Giudecca (right) and to the monastery island of San Giorgio Maggiore (left).

Gondolas gliding over the water, and canals, bridges, and narrow passageways leading to secluded squares – there are romantic corners to be found everywhere in Venice, such as here in the district of Castello.

ABOUT THIS BOOK

Once did She hold the gorgeous East in fee;
And was the safeguard of the West: the worth
Of Venice did not fall below her birth,
Venice, the eldest Child of Liberty.

William Wordsworth, *On the Extinction of the Venetian Republic* (1802)

In *A Venetian Reckoning*, a detective novel by the American writer Donna Leon, Commissario Brunetti's dogged struggle against criminality in Venice is perhaps not written for the faint-hearted, but the photographers and writers of this guide would interpret the title in another way: any reckoning with Venice must lead to the realization that this is simply the most beautiful place on earth. Even wanderers who have visited every country, every ocean, and every city, experiencing each to the full in every sense, would choose to return to Venice, this jewel of human civilization, which is a living museum housing incomparable cultural treasures. The people here enjoy a centuries-old reputation as connoisseurs of music, art, and architecture, and are past masters at the art of celebration when the city explodes with a glittering vibrancy during its festivals, including the world-famous Carnival and the Regata Storica. Venice has been charming its visitors for hundreds of years – where else could you drift along winding waterways beneath ancient stone bridges in a gondola? *Osteria* and cafés with sunlit terraces, and shops selling treasures such as Murano glass, carnival masks, and gilded wood – Renaissance and baroque palaces and churches – piazzas and fountains, balconies and terraces... it is hard to choose between its many attractions, the city is a sheer delight.

Venice is one of a new and unique series. *Photo Guides* combine the lavishness of a coffee-table book with the practicality of a travel guide to create the perfect companion for your city visit. There are over 400 high-quality photographs and maps, together with comprehensive information about the essential highlights of the city and its festivals and lifestyle district by district. Features about the city's history, gastronomy, and special cultural events are accompanied by a detailed timeline, guided walks with expert tips for shoppers and diners alike, information on the major museums, and, of course, all the essential addresses. Each *Photo Guide* also includes a detailed city atlas to help you find your way about.

For centuries, the Doge's Palace on the Piazzetta and the towering campanile have majestically welcomed voyagers arriving in Venice by boat.

TIMELINE

THE HIGHLIGHTS

CONTENTS

"Not just magnificent … but more or less devoid of all ugliness"; everything the great Italian expert, Eckart Peterich, said of this wondrous city half a century ago remains just as true today, despite the occasional subsequent building project that has not escaped controversy – perhaps it is even truer now than ever before. Whilst the streams of tourists who throng Venice's alleys and canals are an inconvenience, even to the visitors themselves, it was the tourist trade that prompted investment in the preservation of this miraculous place.

CITY EXPLORER

CITY ATLAS

TIMELINE

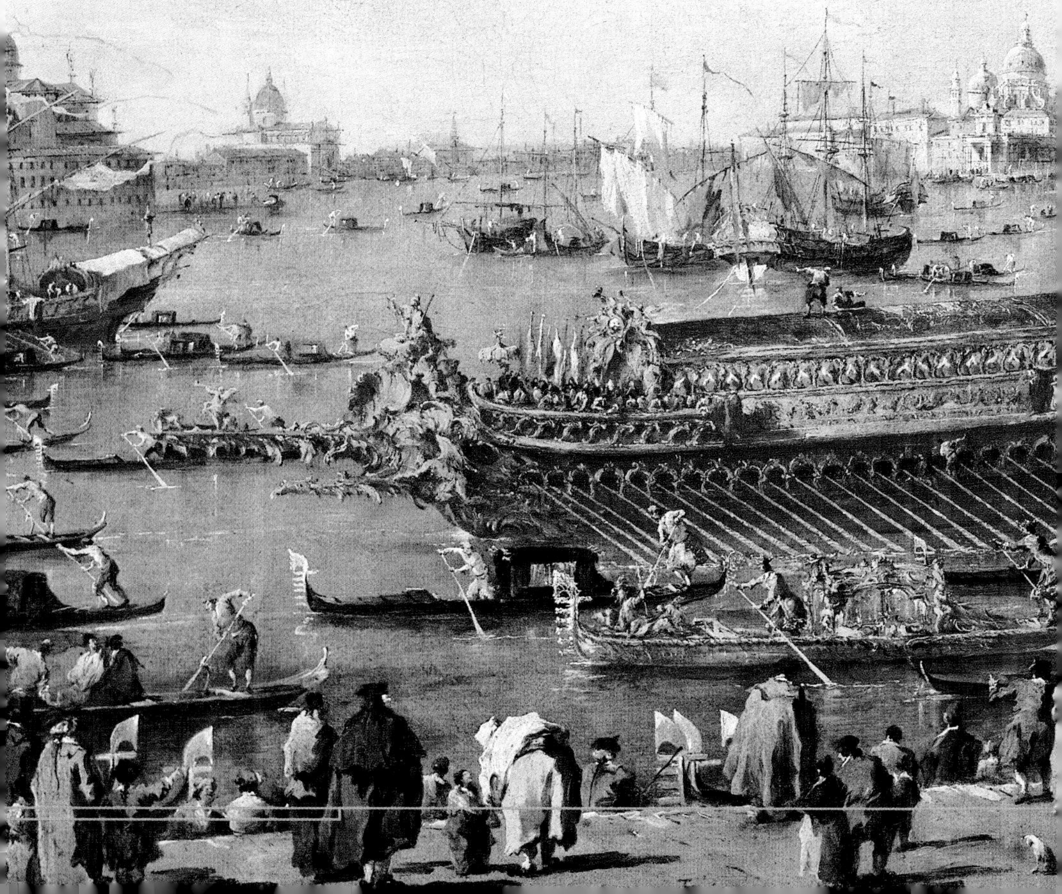

The history of Venice is circumscribed by water: the first settlers sought refuge on the islands in the lagoon in the confusion of a period of mass migration starting in the 4th century. This "gateway to the Adriatic" became the springboard for the city's rise to its position as the leading Mediterranean power in the Middle Ages. Wars with the Turks beginning in the 16th century heralded its decline, and by the 20th century the water literally threatened to submerge its former brilliance. Conservation has prevented such a fate and today Venice is a UNESCO World Heritage Site.

A winged lion with a halo is the emblem of St Mark the Evangelist, who replaced the local St Theodore as Venice's patron saint at the beginning of the 9th century. The Lion of St Mark became the symbol of the Republic's independence and was thus ubiquitous throughout the Eastern Mediterranean, its sovereign territory. Right: This painting in the Sala Grimani of the Doge's Palace was completed by Jacobello Del Fiore in 1415.

Prehistory
The Veneti, who settled here in the first millennium before Christ, give their name to the Veneto.

2nd century BC
After the Veneto has been incorporated into the Roman Empire, the Veneti adopt Roman customs.

313
The Veneto adopts Christianity as its official religion, in line with the entire Roman Empire.

395
The Roman Empire is divided into a western and an eastern empire (Byzantium).

4th–6th century
The Veneto is sacked on numerous occasions in campaigns by Huns, Langobards, and Franks.

697
According to legend, Venice, a Byzantine province since 568, appoints Paoluccio Anafesta as the first doge.

814
First Doge's Palace is built on the Rivo Alto.

828/29
St Mark's alleged remains are brought to Venice from Alexandria.

832
Construction of the first Basilica di San Marco.

1000
Doge Pietro Orseolo celebrates the first *Sposalizio del Mare*.

St Mark, patron saint of Venice

Legend has it that St Mark's missionary journeys brought him to what was to become Venice's lagoon, although it is almost impossible that the saint, who as the first bishop of Alexandria was also founder of the Coptic Church in Egypt, ever actually went there. Nonetheless, St Paul's comrade-in-arms eminently suited the emerging city republic and St Mark's tomb in Alexandria was later looted by Venetian merchants, who brought back his precious bones to their home town. The relics were supposedly transported in a barrel filled with pork to discourage the attentions of Muslim customs officials, who were forbidden to touch it. St Mark (San Marco) became Venice's patron

A 13th-century bronze relief on the high altar in St Mark's Basilica, depicting scenes from the life of the Evangelist.

saint, representing the city's independent claim to power and competing with Peter, Andrew, and Martin, who were revered in Rome, Byzantium, and France respectively. The Evangelist's celebrated symbol, a winged lion, has graced the coat of arms of the city by the lagoon ever since.

The founding of Venice

There is documentary evidence of the foundation of Venice from 25 March 421; it is fair to assume no official foundation took place during the wild times of mass migration.

The mainland by the lagoon, inhabited for centuries by the Veneti, was part of the Roman Empire when the first incursions by Slavic, Germanic, and Gothic tribes began in the 4th century. Such looting and pillaging was too much for a once-proud world power, and the people of the Veneto fled in boats to the islands of the lagoon and the protection afforded them by the surrounding water and marshes.

Christ's blessing – a 12th-century mosaic in the apse of the cathedral of Santa Maria Assunta on Torcello.

Models and original exhibits illustrating Venetian naval history in the Museo Storico Navale.

Byzantium

After the Huns and the Langobards had further disrupted the area in the 5th and 6th centuries, the Venetians placed themselves under the protection of the east Roman Byzantine Empire, which appointed a doge as regent over the lagoon. When the doge's residence in Malamocco on the Lido was sacked by troops under the command of Charlemagne's son, Pippin, the Venetians retreated to the Rivo Alto ("high shore", later known as the Rialto) islands, where first the Doge's Palace and then further buildings were quickly constructed. Charlemagne finally gave up his claim to the Adriatic Sea under the terms of the Peace of Aachen of 812.

Even at this time the Venetians were successful seafarers, and they maintained profitable trade links throughout the Byzantine Empire. In 828 a few brave souls reached Alexandria in Egypt, where they looted the alleged bones of the Apostle Mark. The first basilica in Venice was built to venerate these sacred relics.

PREHISTORY TO
AD **1000**
"The great migrations"
and the founding
of the city

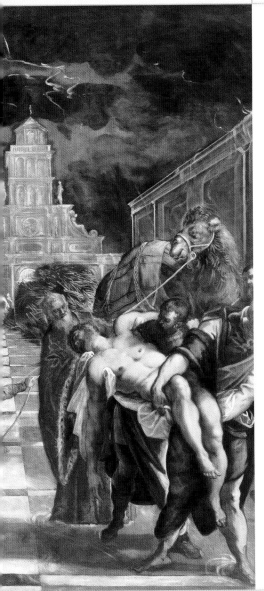

The basis of power

Venice was possessed of a spiritual focus in St Mark and effective temporal power in the doge, who was no longer appointed by Byzantium but elected by the city's leading lagoon with all the wares its population desired.

The *Sposalizio del Mare*, "Marriage with the Sea", was inaugurated in AD 1000. The festival, still celebrated annually, became an expression of Venice's view of itself

Above: This 13th-century mosaic on the exterior of St Mark's Basilica depicts the entry of St Mark the Evangelist's relics into the church.
Left: Episodes from the Evangelist's life are often imaginatively and imposingly recreated in Venice, as here in Tintoretto's *The Stealing of the Dead Body of St Mark* (completed 1566) in the Gallerie dell'Accademia.

families. Shipbuilding rapidly began to flourish, and Venice's fleet had soon subjugated parts of modern-day Croatia and driven the pirates from the Adriatic. This was a prerequisite for the success of the merchant ships that were to supply the as a major sea power. The vital role played by the water in the life of the Republic was symbolized by a ring, thrown into the lagoon by the doge. Today it is the mayor of Venice, accompanied by various dignitaries, who carries out the ceremony.

In this painting by Francesco Bassano (1549–1592), Pope Alexander III is shown handing the holy sword of office to Doge Sebastiano Ziani in 1174 (right). A picture by Antonio Vassilachi (1556–1629) shows Doge Enrico Dandolo crowning Balduin of Flanders as the first emperor of the short-lived Latin Empire after the conquest of Constantinople by the Crusaders in 1204 (far right).

1096–1192
Equipping the first three Crusades with weapons, provisions, and ships turns into a profitable business for the city republic.

1171
Division of Venice into six *sestieri* (districts).

From 1200
Construction of the first (wooden) Rialto Bridge.

1202
Beginning of the Fourth Crusade; Venice takes a leading role.

1204
Looting of considerable treasures in the sack of Constantinople.

1271–1295
Legendary journey to China by the Venetian merchant, Marco Polo.

1284
Introduction of the Venetian gold ducat.

Around 1300
Growth of population to *circa* 100,000 inhabitants.

1309
Construction begins of the modern Palazzo Ducale (Doge's Palace).

1310
Constitutional reform: the doge concedes much of his authority to the newly formed Council of Ten.

1380
Victory of the Venetian fleet over Genoa at Chioggia; Venice now rules the Adriatic.

Marco Polo

Did the adventurer and explorer Marco Polo (*c.* 1254–1324) really travel to China with his father and his uncle? This has recently been called into question, as not a single Chinese source records any Venetian visiting the Middle Kingdom. Marco Polo's *Le divisament dou monde* tells of the

Onward to China: Marco Polo's departure from Venice (book illustration, *c.* 1340).

"wonders of the world" in East Asia and maintains that he lived in China for 17 years, rising to the rank of prefect to Kublai Khan. All that is certain is that Marco Polo was the scion of a Venetian merchant family and had business connections with Asia; whether he made it to China is at best uncertain. It is possible that his knowledge of China, which seems not always to correspond to actual events, was obtained from the reports of other voyagers rather than from personal experience. Nevertheless, Marco Polo has become the epitome of long-distance wanderers, as well as a powerful inspiration for many later journeys.

Christian against Christian: the Crusaders took Constantinople in 1204 (painting by Palma il Giovane, 1587).

The growth of Venice

The 11th century saw the beginning of Venice's ascent as one of the greatest powers in the Mediterranean region. This success was based on four principles: the Republic had excellent relations with both Byzantium and the Holy Roman Empire, treating with both as well as cleverly playing each off against the other. Secondly, the Republic's sea trade led to a growing prosperity that only increased over time. Thirdly, the position of the city in the lagoon was excellent protection against enemy attack, and in contrast to many cities of the time Venice was spared destruction and sacking. Lastly, the city profited a good deal from the Crusades, becoming the preferred supplier of military supplies and especially ships.

War and peace

The Republic did not become actively involved in campaigning in the Holy Land until the Fourth Crusade (1202–04), but even then the Venetians had other things in mind rather than the capture of Egypt.

Under the command of the doge, Enrico Dandolo, Venice's fleet succeeded first in capturing the town of Zara (Zadar) in Dalmatia and then went on to conquer the richest city in the known world: Constantinople. Plundering the capital of the Byzantine Empire in 1204 brought

In 1580 Paolo Veronese painted *Return of the Doge Andrea Contarini after the Victory at Chioggia* for the Doge's Palace. Venice had defeated Genoa and now ruled the Adriatic.

Procession on St Mark's Square (painting by Gentile Bellini, 1496).

The Relic of the Holy Cross is Offered to the Scuola Di S. Giovanni Evangelista (painting by Lazzaro Bastiani, *c.* 1500).

great riches and art treasures into the possession of the Venetians, for example the gilded bronze statues of horses that grace St Mark's Basilica (nowadays replicas, the originals are in the Museo Marciano, inside the Basilica). Byzantine territory was divided up and the Latin Empire established. Large areas of the Aegean were now beholden to Venice.

La Serenissima

Such a degree of power attracted much envy. Genoa, another seafaring republic, felt threatened by Venice's ambition and the tension between the two powers initially found an outlet in small but violent skirmishes. In 1380, however, the situation escalated: Genoa despatched its fleet in the direction of the lagoon, where it was met and annihilated by the Venetians at Chioggia. Venice, now the undisputed ruler of the Adriatic, became known as La Serenissima, "the most serene".

Dynastic rule

This newly acquired wealth had domestic repercussions: the city's leading families demanded political power, which they received in the constitutional reforms of 1310. The newly convened Council of Ten now took decisions that had previously been the responsibility of the doge alone. The city's nobility had long considered itself a social group apart and inau-

gurated the Golden Book (1325), a register in which only the most noble families could be entered. It became the official list of those who could vote or hold office.

Booty from the Fourth Crusade: this porphyry sculpture of the Tetrarchs (four Roman emperors) from the late classical period was brought to Venice after the sacking of Constantinople.

Venice's aristocracy was not the only group to organize itself as a social class in the 13th century: its merchants formed lay brotherhoods, similar to guilds. The focus of each fraternity was the *scuola*, a charitable institution, caring for the sick and feeding the destitute, which looked after the poorest population of the district. The *scuole* were dedicated to saints and increased the social prestige of the fraternity, who erected prestigious buildings, almost like palaces. They also provided an opportunity for non-noble citizens from many different ethnicities and occupations to exercise some degree of power.

An impressive tableau (from left, with regnal years in brackets): this gallery of selected Venetian heads of state from the 15th to the 19th centuries shows the doges Francesco Foscari (1423–57), Giovanni Mocenigo (1478–85), Leonardo Loredan (1501–21), Francesco Donàs (1545–53), Alvise Mocenigo I (1570–77), Marcantonio Memmo (1612–15), Francesco Erizzo (1631–46), and Francesco Morosini (1688–94).

1453
Constantinople is taken by the Turks. Venice is cut off from its trade routes.

1489
Cyprus is brought under Venetian rule.

1504–1516
War of the League of Cambrai against Venice.

1516
Banishment of Jews to the Ghetto – the district known as the "foundry" or, in Venetian dialect, getto or ghetto.

1570
Conquest of Cyprus by the Turks.

1571
A Christian fleet under command of the Venetians defeats the Turks at the sea battle of Lepanto.

1575
An outbreak of plague claims 50,000 victims.

1588
Construction begins on the modern Rialto Bridge.

c. 1600
The number of inhabitants reaches some 150,000.

1630
Plague haunts Venice, costing 100,000 lives.

1669
Crete is conquered by the Turks.

1718
Venice relinquishes control of the Peloponnese to the Turks.

Venice's rule on the mainland

It might be said that the Veneto was La Serenissima's domestic power base – the plain behind the lagoon had been under Venetian control from the earliest times.

At the height of its power, Venice's sovereign territory reached as far as Padua and Vicenza, encompassing the area around Verona to Lake Garda and the northern part of the Veneto, the foothills of the Dolomites. Diverting the River Brenta into the Brenta Canal in the 16th century promoted domestic trade, allowing agricultural produce to be exported to the coast and fish to be brought far inland. The aristocracy used the canal for pleasure cruises while cargo was transported on barges called *burci*.

Venice's formerly immense influence on the mainland is

View of a Town at the Brenta, a painting by Canaletto, 1750.

still discernible in the many prestigious buildings in the cities of Padua, Vicenza, and Verona, which took Venetian building as their architectural model.

United against Turkish expansionism: the victory of a combined Venetian, Spanish, and papal fleet over Ottoman sea power at the

Lion of St Mark vs the Crescent Moon

Unchecked Venetian power in the eastern Mediterranean did not last even a century. In 1453 the Turks conquered Constantinople and brought a large part of the previously Venetian-controlled territory under the rule of the Ottoman Empire.

A Christian fleet under command of the Venetians succeeded in defeating the Turkish fleet at Lepanto in 1571, but this changed little. Cyprus had fallen to the Turks the previous year, and in 1669 Crete was to be taken, followed by the Peloponnese in 1718.

La Serenissima's decline – whilst taking some three centuries – was unstoppable. The discovery of America and the sea route to India also shifted the focus of world trade; it resulted in Venice losing its grip on the highly profitable monopoly on the Levant spice trade.

Beyond the zenith

Venice's glory had begun to crumble quite early, even in the lagoon itself. Whilst it had succeeded in subjugating large parts of the Veneto, even taking towns like Padua

The Doge Pietro Loredan Thanks the Madonna for Delivering Venice from the Plague – a votive picture from 1581, expressing Venetian piety.

and Verona and becoming the third-largest city in Europe (after Paris and

battle of Lepanto in 1571 merely prolonged the gradual decline of Venice.

Naples), it soon encountered stiff resistance. Several European powers, supported by the emperor and the pope, formed the League of Cambrai in 1504 and conducted a campaign against Venice that lasted until 1516. Whilst ultimately unsuccessful, the campaign seriously weakened both sides, a situation only compounded by two plague epidemics that claimed many victims in 1575 and 1630.

At the same time as many other Mediterranean powers were departing to explore the New World and to make their fortunes there, Venice was concerned merely with survival; after several high storm tides, large walls (*murazzi*) were constructed at the lagoon entrances.

Degenerate beauty

Sometimes it can take a period of decline, a sense of living at the end of an era – the *fin de siècle* – to bring

the arts truly into bloom, and thus Venice's most beautiful buildings and artwork came about between the 15th and the 18th centuries. La Serenissima's wealth in the High Renaissance and the baroque periods was spent on the works of Titian and Tintoretto, Veronese and Palladio, and the Tiepolos, father and son. Whilst Venice did not lose its position as the pre-eminent patron of the arts until the rococo period, palaces and churches were decaying, symptoms of a city that almost literally was "going under".

The lagoon has since displayed a kind of degenerate charm, a melancholy that inspired Thomas Mann's novella *Death in Venice* (published 1912, adapted into a film by Visconti in 1970) and Daphne du Maurier's evocative short story *Don't Look Now* (1971), adapted by Nicolas Roeg for his atmospheric and highly charged 1973 film classic.

Palaces on the water

The greatest architectural achievement in the construction of Venice's enormous palaces and churches has nothing to do with their size or their façades, but rather lies hidden underwater, in their foundations. Even to make construction on the soft ground near the canals possible, a load-bearing surface had to be created, and to this end the once-extensive oak and larch forests of the Veneto and Istria were felled. The tree trunks were driven into the mud of the lagoon, either in bundles or closely packed, and covered over with horizontal beams. These wooden piles did not rot, as bacteria that might cause decay cannot live in

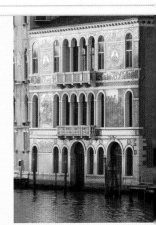

The 16th-century Palazzo Barbarigo, decorated with mosaics added in 1887.

"float": mosaic tiles and terrace flagstones, for example,

An unusual viewpoint: in 1640 Joseph Heintz painted this bird's-eye view of Venice (on display in the Museo Civico Correr, Venice).

the salty waters of the lagoon, but they did move slightly in the current like a boat. For this reason the floors in the buildings were laid so that they could

were laid on a wooden base which sat on the beams, and could move in time with the whole building, giving the odd sensation of being at sea while on land.

Sketches of Venice (from left): in the 18th century, the lagoon was a stage for festivals and carnivals, a place of masks and disguises, as seen here in Pietro Longhi's painting, *Il Ridotto di Ca Giustiniani*; the 1797 caricature in the middle depicts the all-conquering Napoleon Bonaparte as a quack doctor in Venice; Vincenzo Chilone's painting *The Return of the Horses of San Marco 1815*.

1748
After the end of the War of the Austrian Succession, territories around Venice fall to Austria.

1796
During its Italian campaign, the French army defeats the Austrians at the Battle of Lodi.

1797
Napoleon exchanges Venice for Lombardy; the lagoon is now under Austrian rule.

1804/05
Napoleon returns to Venice as emperor of France and king of Italy.

1815
The Final Act of the Congress of Vienna places Venice under Austrian rule.

1845
Construction of the Ponte della Libertà railway bridge makes Venice accessible by land.

1848/49
First Italian War of Independence; the Austrians are swept from Venice.

1859
Second Italian War of Independence under the leadership of Giuseppe Garibaldi.

1861
Victor Emanuel II becomes the first king of a united Italy, a title he held until his death in 1878.

1866
Venice and the Veneto are made part of the kingdom.

San Lazzaro degli Armeni

One of the most significant bases for Armenian religion and culture outside its

The order's refectory in Pier Antonio Novelli's painting *The Last Supper*.

homeland lies west of the Lido. The island of San Lazzaro, dedicated to the patron saint of lepers, was initially used as a quarantine station and leper colony. After a short period of settlement by the Dominicans in the 16th century, the Armenian monk, Mekhitar of Sivas, and several of his fellow brothers founded a monastery on the island in 1717 after fleeing persecution in Venice. Today the monastery is the headquarters of the Mekhitarist order in the Armenian Catholic rite. Particularly open to literature and the arts, the order amassed a large collection of Armenian and Oriental artwork, manuscripts, and books of great cultural and historical significance, which can still be viewed today. The English poet Lord Byron, who had lived in Venice since 1816, spent six months at the monastery studying Armenian.

A backdrop for interesting times (from top): the 1797 history painting *The Abdication of the Doge Ludovico Manin* takes as its subject the Napoleonic era, which had repercussions not just for Venice; the Sala Canoviana in the Ala Napoleonica; freedom fighters storm the Arsenale in 1848, a stage in the Venetian struggle against Habsburg rule.

The last doge

On 12 May 1797, Venice's Great Council convened for the last time in the Doge's Palace, to accept the abdication of the 120th and last doge of Venice, Ludovico Manin. Venice had been ruled by the doges (Venetian dialect, *cf* Italian *duce*, English *duke*) from around 700. Elected for life by the aristocracy, they were normally drawn from among the city's elders. Remuneration for the position was not large, so most doges also engaged in trade. But by 1797, this ancient office, along with the Republic, had ceased to exist, falling victim, like much of Europe at the time, to the Napoleonic Wars.

Taking overall command of the French Revolutionary Army in 1796, Napoleon had beaten the Austrians and the Piedmontese, and conquered Milan. Just a year later he stood at the gates of a Venice that was barely capable of offering resistance. After the abdication of the doge, Napoleon looted the city, and the Golden Book, the symbol of dynastic rule, was burnt. He subsequently gave Habsburg Austria control of Venice, swapping it for Lombardy.

Napoleon again

In 1805, Napoleon returned to Venice. A year previously he had declared himself emperor of France and, after several campaigns against Austria, he became king of Italy on 26 May 1805.

French rule in Venice was particularly harsh for spiritual institutions: monastic orders were disbanded and monasteries and churches dissolved, and their possessions confiscated.

However, the emperor's rule over the lagoon was at an end in less than ten years, after the defeat of the French army at Leipzig and Waterloo. The peace treaty negotiated at the Congress of Vienna (1814–15) made the Austrians the new rulers of Venice.

The road to Italy

Industrialization began under Austrian rule: gas lighting was introduced; a free port was built in 1830; and the Liberty Bridge (Ponte della Libertà) and Santa Lucia railway station were constructed in 1845.

The corollary of such progress was, as elsewhere, the impoverishment of large sections of the population and growing dissatisfaction with those in power. A wave of civil and nationalist unrest that was sweeping Europe in 1848 culminated in the Apennine peninsula in the First Italian War of Independence, and for about a year Venice was in a position to assert its independence under the leadership of Daniele Manin (1804–1857). It subsequently reverted to Austrian rule, which was finally ended in the Second Italian War of Independence that had raged since 1859. The Kingdom of Italy, proclaimed in 1861 under King Victor Emanuel II, joined the Prussians in their war with Habsburg Austria in 1866. After a plebiscite had been held, Venice joined the new Italian nation-state as part of the Veneto.

A town of festivals

Hardly a month goes by in Venice without a feast day or festival.

The largest of these are world famous and attract hundreds and thousands of tourists to the city: Venice Carnival in February or March; the film festival in September; and the annually alternating, late summer attraction of the art or architecture Biennale. Other kinds of attractions recall the Republic's eventful seafaring history: the Marriage with the Sea, also called the Festa della Sensa, held on the Sunday after Ascension, is a mighty procession of historic gondolas along the Grand Canal. The Regata Storica, which culminates in a

Pure pageantry: the Regata Storica on the Grand Canal.

celebrations take place. Twice a year, in July and November, the grand processions of the Festa del Reden-

in traditional costumes taking part in the spectacle. St Mark's Day, 25 April, is a special feast, on which every Venetian gives his partner a red rose and many public

Carnival masks of cult status and yet with a slightly eerie feel: a couple in traditional *maschera nobile*.

regatta of various boat classes held on the first Sunday in September, is also staged here, with the *Bucintoro*, the doge's prestigious ship of state, and hundreds of historic boats with crews

tore and the Festa della Saluta commemorate those who died of the plague in Venice. On the eve of the Festa del Redentore, a firework display lights up the night sky for almost an hour.

A cultural hothouse for foreign talent (from left): Ernest Hemingway loved Venice and the lagoon, making it the setting for the novel *Across the River and Into the Trees*; the art collector Peggy Guggenheim bought a *palazzo* and lived there for 30 years; Donna Leon, author of famous crime novels set in Venice, is also an American; the entrepreneur François Pinault collected great art – in Venice, of course.

1895
The first Art Biennale welcomes visitors to Venice.

1902
The campanile, the bell tower of St Mark's, collapses (and is reconstructed in 1912).

1912
Thomas Mann's novella *Death in Venice (Der Tod in Venedig)* is published.

1917
The port of Marghera is constructed, along with plants for heavy industry.

1932
The first International Film Festival takes place on the Lido.

1939–1945
World War II; Venice escapes unscathed.

1960
Venice's Marco Polo airport opens in Tessera.

1966
Great flood in the lagoon, which rises by 2 m (6.5 feet). 5,000 are made homeless and countless works of art are destroyed or damaged.

c. **1970**
Venice has 350,000 inhabitants, the highest number recorded.

2004
Work on the MOSE water regulation project begins.

2008
Santiago Calatrava's Constitution Bridge over the Grand Canal is completed.

Acqua alta

Countless folded duckboards have been distributed across the city and lie in wait, ready to be set up during *acqua alta*, the seasonal floods. The first record of a flood dates back to the end of the 6th century. Subsidence due to repeated industrial use of groundwater, dredging the port entrances, the silting up of the canals, and global warming are responsible for

On trestles: a scene from a flooded St Mark's Square.

the regularity and the severity of the floods, which have increased markedly in the course of the 20th century. The water level has risen by 12 cm (5 inches) since 1908, and if no action is taken, Venice will sink in the foreseeable future.
The Modulo Sperimentale Elettromeccanico, known as MOSE for short, promises a solution, however. No fewer than 78 hinged barriers are to be attached to the seabed at the entrances to the lagoon. During times of normal sea level they remain closed, but as the water level rises, the hinges are opened to form a dam, preventing seawater from entering the lagoon.

Former glories

By the 20th century, the once serene city had become somewhat of an anachronism in a modern, industrial world. Sea trade continued to decline and the city's industrial production was hampered by the difficulty of delivering raw materials: by boat via the canals, and then by trolley over the

Disaster: on 14 July 1902 the Campanile collapses.

bridges and through the streets. Only the island of La Giudecca was able to offer a foothold for a large industrial bakery and, to a limited extent, other industrial development, such as in the north of Cannaregio. Employment, and thus human activity, became increasingly concentrated on the mainland.
A large port was built at Marghera in 1917, and in 1931 Piazzale Roma was finally completed, connected to the mainland settlement of Mestre by an embanked road. Marco Polo airport, opened in 1960, is also on the mainland, 20 minutes from the heart of the city. The approach on a clear day is quite simply breathtaking.

The aesthetics of decline

More and more Venetian residents were being driven from the lagoon, some journeying great distances; the turn of the 20th century saw many people from Venice and the Veneto forced to flee to America to escape poverty, and living conditions on the islands in the lagoon

Canal full: cruise ships and gondolas rub shoulders.

became increasingly more difficult.
The principal reason for this was that the ever-expanding industrial regions of Mestre and Marghera simply dumped the waste water from their steel mills, foundries, and petrochemical factories into the lagoon. With outbreaks of cholera and a rapidly departing younger population, Venice was slowly becoming a stinking sewer.
The population of the lagoon has shrunk by a third since 1970 and the taxes of the population have increased rapidly. Around 1900, the European upper-middle classes of the *fin de siècle* were entranced by a degen-

erate Romanticism whose manifest expression was seen in the collapse of the elderly campanile of St Mark's in 1902. The morbid charm of this singular city on the water, which could be observed without hazard from the mundane world of the beaches of the Lido, fascinated the *beau monde*; Venice became a sort of inhabited open-air museum, of the lagoon with a system of sluice gates, was begun in 2004. A large-scale schedule of building renovation and canal-cleaning was also initiated. The foul stench that once hung over the city is now only occasionally perceptible to visitors in the summer months.

The Venetians had realized how much capital lay in their past: accommodating and

Hotel Danieli

Not far from the Bridge of Sighs, on the Riva degli Schiavoni, the promenade on the lagoon, lies one of Europe's most exclusive addresses. The building now occupied by the Hotel Danieli was constructed in the 14th century as a palace in the Gothic style for Doge Dandolo. Used as a hotel since 1822, this famous: Honoré de Balzac was indulged in luxury here, as were Charles Dickens and Richard Wagner.

In 1832, the married writer George Sand spent time at the Hotel Danieli with her lover, Alfred de Musset, and their stay, charged with passion and jealousy, became the basis for the 1999 film *Les enfants du siècle*; in 1630 the building also became

A bold curve: the bridge designed by Santiago Calatrava has spanned the Grand Canal since 2008.

A beauty that defies time: elegant columns and arches grace the façade of the former Palazzo Dandolo.

and its role as a tourist destination promised a route out of poverty.

Conservation and recovery

After severe flooding on the lagoon in 1966, caused by the canals gradually becoming silted up, a protest movement was formed, and in 1973 this brought about the first legal measures against water and air pollution and the subsidence of the islands. The lagoon has also been on the UNESCO International Register of Cultural Property under Special Protection since 1987.

The extensive MOSE project, intended to prevent flooding feeding the hordes of tourists who descended from all quarters, offering sightseeing packages, and the sale of souvenirs led to a restructuring of the economy toward the service sector. The money brought into the city by the tourists could be used to conserve Venice's unique artistic treasures as well as their unique setting, but the disadvantages of this development were also apparent: the visitors thronging the narrow streets, especially at weekends, were to find authentic city life only in the suburbs.

Low-rent kitsch was to flourish amongst the Renaissance and baroque architectural masterpieces. three-floor building with its striking pink façade and exquisite interior décor has become a destination of choice for the rich and part of musical history with Claudio Monteverdi's production of *Proserpina rapita*, the first opera performance in Venice.

Let there be light: the Murano glass chandeliers in the foyer are all handmade.

Great minds think alike: Balzac, Proust, and George Sand all stayed here.

SAN MARCO

St Mark's Basilica and Palazzo Ducale (Doge's Palace) have made San Marco *sestiere* the spiritual and temporal hub of Venice for centuries. Bounded on three sides by the magnificent Grand Canal and on the fourth by Cannaregio, and Castello to the north-east, this district, named after the city's patron saint, remains the focal point of the city to this day and attracts tourists in their thousands. Its most impressive buildings are on the south bank, with a view from Piazzetta San Marco over the lagoon – a panorama that cannot be equalled.

1 St Mark's Square

2 Torre dell'Orologio

3 Museo Civico Correr

4 Piazzetta di San Marco
   Biblioteca Marciana

5 St Mark's Basilica

6 Doge's Palace

7 Bridge of Sighs

8 Around Campo
   San Moisè

9 Teatro La Fenice

10 Chiesa di San Salvador

11 Palazzo Contarini
   del Bovolo

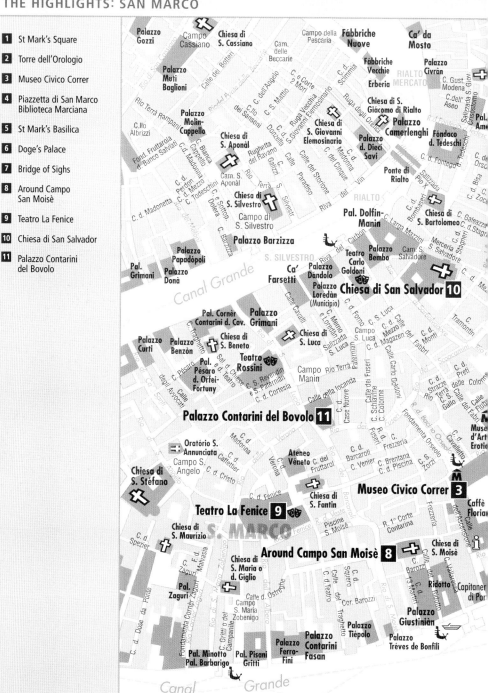

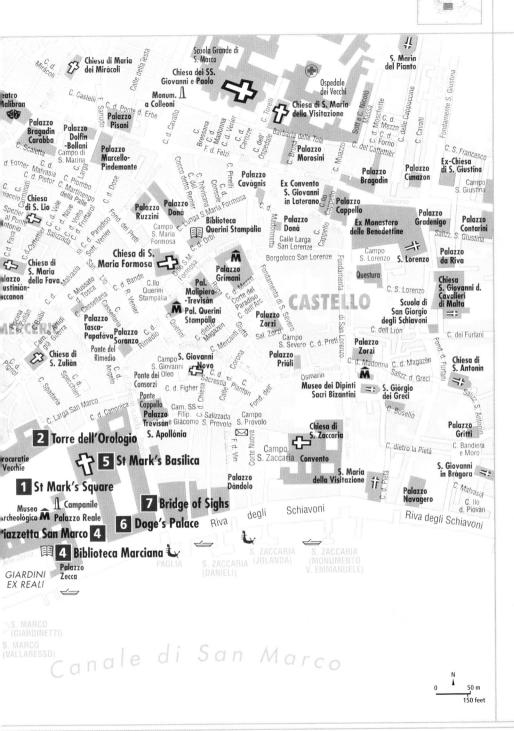

Chiesa di Maria dei Mirácoli

Scuola Grande di S. Marco

Chiesa dei SS. Giovanni e Paolo

S. Maria del Pianto

C. d. Mirácoli

eatro
Malibran

C. Castelli

F. Sando

C. d. Ponte d. Erbe

Monum. a Colleoni

Ospedale dei Vecchi

Chiesa di S. Maria della Visitazione

Sott e C. Nicolò

Fondamente S. Giustina

Palazzo Bragadin Carabba

Palazzo Dolfin -Bollani

Palazzo Pisani

C. d. Cavallo

Bressana

C. d. Madonna

C. del Venier

C. delle Carozze

C. del Ospedale

Barbara delle Tole

Massa

Moschette

C. d. Mezzo

C. d. delle Cappucine

C. Cavatti

C. S. Francesco

C. Scaletta

Campo di S. Marina

Palazzo Marcello-Pindemonte

C. Bressana

F. d. Felzi

C. Pinelli

C. del

C. d. Brusa

C. d. Muazzo

C. d. Forno

C. del Caffettièr

Palazzo Morosini

Ex-Chiesa di S. Giustina

d. Forner

Malvasia

C. d. Pistor

C. Piombo

C. Martinengo

della Palle

Palazzo Cavágnis

Ex Convento S. Giovanni in Laterano

Palazzo Bragadin

Palazzo Cimazon

Campo S. Giustina

iacciol

Chiesa di S. Lio

Spezier al Ponte

C. d. Cafettier

Salizzada

C. d. Paradiso

C. d. Vele

C. d. Nave

C. d. Volto

C. d. Frutariol

Fond. dei Preti

C. d. Dose

C. Martinengo

C. Trevisana

C. d. Console

C. Cocco dietro Renier

C. d. Lunga S Maria Formosa

Palazzo Ruzzini

Palazzo Donà

Biblioteca Querini Stampália

Palazzo Donà

Palazzo Cappello

Ex Monastero delle Benedettine

Palazzo Gradenigo

Palazzo Contarini

Salizz. S. Giustina

Antonio

Chiesa di S. Maria della Fava

Campo S. Maria Formosa

C. Madonnetta

Calle Larga San Lorenzo

C. d. Cappello

Campo S. Lorenzo

S. Lorenzo

Palazzo da Riva

alazzo ustinián-accanon

C. d. Mussato

C. di Tosca

C. d. Bande

C. R. Venier

Chiesa di S. Maria Formosa

Palazzo Grimani

Ruga

Giuffa

Corte del Paradiso

Borgoloco San Lorenzo

Questura

Fondamenta di S. Severo

Campo S. Lorenzo

C. S. Lorenzo

Chiesa S. Giovanni d. Cavalieri di Malta

MERCERIA

C. Zulian

C. Balbi

C. Cassellaria

C. Cassellaria

Palazzo Tasca-Papafáva

Palazzo Soranzo

Ponte del Rimedio

C. d. Rimedio

C. Querini

Pal. Malipiero -Trevisàn

Pal. Querini Stampália

Palazzo Zorzi

Fondamenta di S. Severo

Scuola di San Giorgio degli Schiavoni

C. dell Lión

C. dei Furlani

CASTELLO

Cam. Antidi già Guerra

Chiesa di S. Zulián

Ponte del Rimedio

C. d. Angelo

Campo S. Giovanni

S. Giovanni Novo

C. dietro Magazen

C. d. Mercanti

Corona

C. Provolo

Sal. Zorzi

Palazzo Priúli

Palazzo Zorzi

C. d. Madonna

C. d. Preti

C. d. Magazén

Salizz. d. Greci

Chiesa di S. Antonin

C. d. Pignol

C. d. Specchieri

C. Spadaria

Ponte del Oleo

Consorzi

C. d. Figher

Ponte Cappello

C. d. Chiesa

Sacrestia

C. d. Pianton

Osmarin

Museo dei Dipinti Sacri Bizantini

S. Giorgio dei Greci

Salizz. S. Antonin

C. Larga San Marco

C. d. Canonica

Cam. SS. Filip.

Palazzo Trevisàn

Salizzada S. Provolo

Campo S. Provolo

C. d. dell

Fond.

Chiesa di S. Zaccaria

C. Bosello

Palazzo Gritti

2 Torre dell'Orologio

5 St Mark's Basilica

1 St Mark's Square

7 Bridge of Sighs

6 Doge's Palace

4 Biblioteca Marciana

rocuratie Vecchie

S. Apollónia

Campo S. Zaccaria

Convento

S. Maria della Visitazione

C. dietro la Pietà

C. Bandiera e Moro

S. Giovanni in Brágora

C. Malvasiá

Museo archeológico

Campanile

Palazzo Reale

Piazzetta San Marco

Palazzo Dándolo

F. d. Vin

Corte Nuova

Riva

degli

Schiavoni

Palazzo Navagero

C. d. Pietà

C. Ilo d. Piován

Palazzo Zecca

GIARDINI EX REALI

PAGLIA

S. ZACCARIA (DANIELI)

S. ZACCARIA (JOLANDA)

S. ZACCARIA (MONUMENTO V. EMMANUELE)

Riva degli Schiavoni

S. MARCO (GIARDINETTI)

S. MARCO (VALLARESSO)

Canale di San Marco

N
0   50 m
150 feet

THE HIGHLIGHTS: SAN MARCO

St Mark's is the only square in Venice to be called a *piazza* – each of the others is called a *campo*. The Ala Napoleonica has the most beautiful view of the Basilica and the Campanile (below). Below right: The colonnades of the elegant Procuratie.

In the evenings, an illuminated St Mark's Square hosts small coffee-house orchestras playing, at times, first-class, light classical music. The prices in the cafés, which are steep to begin with, are then augmented with a further, no less ambitious extra charge; standing places in the square are, of course, free.

Piazza San Marco has stood proudly in front of St Mark's Basilica (Basilica di San Marco) since the 9th century; it has been shaped by the centuries during which it was the backdrop for Venice's festivals, processions, and public events. To the east lie the Basilica and the Campanile, while the north and south sides adjoin the majestic 16th-century administrative buildings of the Procuratie. The western side is closed by the Ala Napoleonica, which was constructed as a residence on the orders of the conquering Napoleon Bonaparte in 1810. Visitors wishing to experience what Napoleon called the "most beautiful drawing room in Europe" in style should visit one of the coffee houses from which gentle classical music flows. You'll experience a wonderful view of the 12th-century campanile, the Basilica's bell tower, which collapsed in 1902 but was rebuilt within a decade.

The famous Caffè Florian in the Procuratie Nuove colonnades was given its modern form in 1858. Each of its small rooms is decorated with a different theme (below). Lying diagonally opposite, the Gran Caffè Quadri was established in 1775 and is equally well known (right).

CAPPUCCINOS AND WALTZES: CAFFÈ FLORIAN AND CO.

People have been drinking coffee in Venice since 1615. This aromatic luxury product found its way to the lagoon from the Orient via Constantinople only a few years after the arrival of tea, and the first Venetian *bottega del caffè* appeared around the middle of the 17th century. Floriano Francesconi opened the Alla Venezia Trionfante, later called the Caffè Florian, in 1720, and this coffee house on St Mark's Square soon became one of the most famous and expensive in the world. Initially it was frequented by the nobility, but then artists and intellectuals found their way inside; the writers Goethe and Balzac spent time here, as did the English painter William Turner, the composers Verdi, Wagner, and Liszt, and novelists such as Mark Twain, Proust, Thomas Mann, and Hemingway. Other venues with similarly imposing interiors, such as Lavena and Quadri, soon established themselves in the vicinity of Florian's. The charm that attracts visitors today was developed in the Habsburg era; the establishments served as a venue for social intercourse and reading the newspapers, and soon bands were providing appropriate background music. The Viennese works of Johann Strauss, both the elder and younger, are still to be heard wherever visitors delight in relaxing to the sound of waltz music.

THE HIGHLIGHTS: SAN MARCO

TIP Cenedese

Horse's hoof: the view from the gallery of St Mark's, where Venice's famous Byzantine gilded bronze horses (copies of the originals) stand, to the entrance of the Museo Civico Correr. Beneath the Torre dell'Orologio is the entrance to the Mercerie dell'Orologia and its upmarket stores (below right).

A good selection of Murano glassware can be found in the traditional Cenedese store. The founder, Gino Cenedese, was an apprentice glassblower from an early age and each piece is still lovingly hand-crafted.
Piazza San Marco 40/41;
Tel (041) 73 98 77;
Mon–Sat 9.30–12.30, 15.00–20.00.

The Torre dell'Orologio, a clock tower located to the left of the main façade of St Mark's, was built over a Renaissance portal at the end of the 15th century and extended by one level in the 18th century. It is topped with a bell struck on the complete hours by two statues of Moors. Every Epiphany (6 January), the figures of the Three Kings proceed across the golden dial. The Museo Civico Correr is housed in the Ala Napoleonica (the Napoleonic Wing) and the Procuratie Nuove. The museum documents the history of Venice, but is not just a destination for fans of old prints, coins, weapons, and relics of the doges – the museum also boasts a first class art collection, including works by the Bellini family, some of the most important Venetian painters of the fifteenth century (see p. 184).

Below: Wisps of fog and the light of dawn create an unreal atmosphere on the Piazzetta, with the Doge's Palace and San Giorgio Maggiore church in the background, entirely fitting for the visit of a three-masted tall ship. Right: the colonnades of the Biblioteca Marciana, whose interior conceals a wealth of sculptures and paintings.

Libreria Sansovino is a treasure trove of art books, rarities, and second-hand books. The bookshop, located under the arcades at the entrance to the tiny gondola mooring of Bacino Orseolo, has been selling books here for around a hundred years.
San Marco 84; Tel (041) 522 26 23.

The part of the Piazza between the Doge's Palace and the Biblioteca Marciana is known as the Piazzetta San Marco. Here the large ships bearing diplomatic envoys would land, their aristocratic passengers disembarking to be led into the Palace. The new arrivals' view of St Mark's and the clock tower was framed by two granite pillars topped with the symbols of the Republic's sovereignty: the Colonne di Marco e Teodoro are crowned with statues of the Lion of St Mark and St Theodore – the old and the new patron saints, as it were. Legend has it that Doge Michele brought the columns back from the Lebanon in 1125. The Doge's Palace lies to the right, and to the left there is the Biblioteca Marciana, constructed in the 16th century by Jacopo Sansovino in a Roman Renaissance style. Its sumptuous rooms house a significant collection of Greek, Latin, and Oriental manuscripts.

Imagination knows no limits in in terms of Venice Carnival's masks and costumes. Traditional masks have always played an important role, and many date back to the Commedia dell'Arte, with characters such as Pulcinella, Arlecchino, and Pantalone. The most important historical mask is the *bautta* (far right), which is also worn on certain special occasions outside Carnival.

Only the carnivals of Rio de Janeiro and Cologne can rival that of Venice. Flocks of tourists converge on the city every year and fantastically costumed figures throng the squares, either attending select and stylish masked balls or watching live performances or even puppet shows. This great traditional celebration was first documented in the 13th century, and over the years ever more elaborate ways of marking the days before the beginning of Lent have been developed. Reaching its peak on Shrove Tuesday, the festival's reputation as the epitome of unbridled exoticism and eroticism was established in the 17th and 18th centuries. The hedonistic festival was banned for years under Napoleonic rule, and only in recent decades has the Venice Carnival regained its former glory. Venetian masquerade is unique throughout the world and has its origins in the costumes of traditional Commedia dell'Arte, whose typical accessories include the *bautta*, a kind of hood, or the *volto* or *larva*, a white or black papier-mâché mask covering the upper half of the face; gentlemen may also choose to wear a tricorne hat and ladies a feathered fascinator. The creation of these extremely elaborate costumes led to the establishment of the *maschereri*, a separate profession of "mask-maker".

THE HIGHLIGHTS: SAN MARCO

INFO Views

The richly decorated façade of St Mark's Basilica, with its shining golden mosaics, pillared portals, Gothic tabernacles, and statues draws every gaze on St Mark's Square. This former doge's chapel was also the state church of the Republic and is the most important medieval building in Venice.

The panorama from the viewing platform on the Campanile reveals the unique shape of the city and the lagoon. An elevator speeds visitors to a height of 100 m (328 feet).
Piazza San Marco; Easter–June 9.00–19.00, July–Sept 9.00–21.00, Oct 9.00–19.00, Nov–Easter 9.30–15.45, daily

Construction of the Basilica di San Marco was begun in the 11th century on the site of two former buildings. Mimicking the Church of the Holy Apostles in Constantinople, its floor plan is in the form of a Greek cross whose center and arms are each topped with a cupola. The Oriental feel of the church came about in a second building phase after Venice was conquered by Byzantium. The church was given Gothic features between the 14th and 16th centuries. The façade, concealing an entrance hall, is divided into five arched portals with mosaics in the Byzantine tradition incorporating war booty won by the city. The legendary Horses of St Mark, giant gilded bronze equine statues, are situated above this in a gallery; the originals were looted from Constantinople by the Venetians in 1204. The four side arches behind the gallery are also decorated with mosaics.

THE HIGHLIGHTS: SAN MARCO

The golden mosaics of St Mark's glittering interior are magnificent. The presbytery is divided by the iconostasis, an altar screen built between 1394 and 1404, and richly decorated with statues (below). The Museo Marciano in the Basilica houses the originals of the bronze horses on the façade, where they have been replaced by copies (below right).

INFO Holy Mass

Mass in the Basilica is more uplifting than the hordes of tourists outside. Sunday Mass is especially solemn and often enhanced with moving choral music.

Piazza San Marco; Tel (041) 522 56 97; 7.00, 8.00, 9.00, 11.00, 12.00 (except July and Aug), and 18.45, daily, Sun also 17.30

St Mark's is unique primarily because of its mosaics. More than 4,000 sq. m (43,000 sq. feet) of mosaic work was completed in the 12th and 13th centuries, adorning the cupola domes, the walls, and the entrance hall; gold was chosen throughout for the backgrounds of the mosaics. The oldest mosaic, in the cupola in front of the crossing, depicts the miracle of Pentecost; the middle cupola shows the Ascension of Christ, the northernmost shows the life of St John the Evangelist, and the southernmost the lives of Saints Nicholas, Clement, Blasius, and Leonard, whose alleged relics were housed in the basilica. The Emanuel Dome shows Christ, flanked by Mary and the prophets, giving a blessing, and beneath this is the famous Pala d'Oro. This altar retable is a masterpiece of the goldsmith's art, incorporating hundreds of enamel tiles and precious stones.

THE HIGHLIGHTS: SAN MARCO

The façade of the Doge's Palace combines Gothic elements with Byzantine
and Arabic forms. The delicate arcade
beneath is followed by a loggia with
cusped arches and decorative pierced
quatrefoils. The magnificent top floor is
punctuated with ogival windows.

The Palazzo Ducale served not only as the doge's residence, but also as a town hall, courthouse, and prison. It received its current form, with three wings, in the 15th century. To the left of the balustrade, next to the Basilica, is the Porta della Carta, the "paper gate"; ordinary citizens could submit pleas and requests in writing here, hence its name. The inner courtyard of the palace is graced by the Arco Foscari, reminiscent of Roman triumphal arches, and the Scala dei Giganti, a magnificent staircase topped with giant statues. One of the world's largest paintings is to be found inside: Tintoretto's *Paradise*, in the Great Council Hall. The magnificent ceiling painting, in praise of La Serenissima, is the work of Paolo Veronese. Further pictures by both artists are in the Sala del Collegio. The Scala d'Oro is also worth seeing, a magnificent staircase with gilded stucco work.

Canaletto's painting of 1750, *The Return of the Bucintoro on Ascension Day*, depicts the doge's magnificent galley amongst festively decorated gondolas in front of the Doge's Palace (below). Titian's 1555 portrait of Doge Francesco Venier is a masterpiece (below right). Right: Doge Francesco Foscari before the Lion of St Mark, the ubiquitous symbol of Venice, located above the late Gothic Porta della Carta, completed in 1442.

THE DOGES

The rule of the doges as city and later state leaders dates back to the 7th century, when Venice was part of the powerful Byzantine Empire. Paoluccio Anafesta supposedly became the first *dux*, the Latin for a military leader, in 697, although the first recorded doge is Orso Ipato, who is documented from 726 onward. He was elected by Venice's patrician dynasties and reigned with absolute power, as did his successors. Constitutional reform in the 12th century transferred many of the privileges of the office to the newly created Council of Ten, after which the doge carried out largely symbolic functions until the abdication of the last incumbent was forced by Napoleon in 1797. The size of the sum of money payable by candidates upon their election restricted the appointment, which was for life, to scions of only the very richest families. The election itself, a complicated process that was changed several times over the centuries, was a public event and took place in St Mark's Square. As a sign of his power, the doge alone was permitted to wear a cap called a *corno* and an ermine cape called a *bavaro*. The equally exclusive right to reside in the Doge's Palace was often only of a short duration; many incumbents of the coveted post soon died an unnatural death.

THE HIGHLIGHTS:
SAN MARCO

Amongst the reliefs adorning the Doge's Palace is the *Drunkenness of Noah* on the corner leading to the Ponte della Paglia (below). The Bridge of Sighs, constructed in the 17th century, leads to the Prigioni Nuove, the slightly eerie 16th-century prison cells (below right).

TIP Al Vecio Penasa

Typical of Venice, this small bar, located almost unnoticed in among the boutiques and restaurants, is where many a local would take an early morning snack, perhaps even allowing himself a beer or prosecco as well.
Calle delle Rasse; Tel (041) 523 72 02; Thurs–Tues 7.00–1.00.

Two parts of the Doge's Palace on the lagoon side are connected by a covered bridge erected in the 16th century. The Ponte dei Sospiri received its popular name, "Bridge of Sighs", because those sentenced in the courthouse of the palace had to cross this bridge to reach the prisons. There were two kinds of prison accommodation: about 20 cells in the damp, stone cellar rooms lying beneath sea level were known as *pozzi* (the Wells); and the six or seven cells in the attic, known as *piombi* (the Leads), were lead-lined and unbearably hot in summer. The most famous person incarcerated in the *piombi* was Giacomo Casanova, the famous adventurer, who was sentenced for blasphemy in 1755, escaping a year later over the roof of the building next door. The covered bridge is made of white limestone and spans the Rio di Palazzo. There are two copies in England, one in Cambridge and the other in Oxford.

Casanova's life has been the basis for countless films. Italy's greatest director, Federico Fellini, shot the most elaborate version in 1976 (below); Donald Sutherland played the lead role (inset, below). Lasse Hallström's 2005 film *Casanova* gave the lead to Heath Ledger (below right). Right: Casanova described his escape from the Leads in his memoirs.

GIACOMO CASANOVA – ADVENTURER AND SCHOLAR

Apart from Marco Polo, the most famous and certainly most vivid figure in Venetian history is Giacomo Casanova (1725–1798). A trained lawyer, he toured Europe as a soldier, musician, theatre director, and secret agent, amongst other things, and is considered the epitome of the adventurer and womanizer. This reputation rests principally on Casanova's own memoirs, written towards the end of his life when he was a librarian to Count Waldstein at Schloss Dux in Bohemia, and which secured his place in world literature. In these memoirs, the author, whose name has since become synonymous throughout the world with the character of a male seducer, recounts how he was forever falling victim to his ruling passions: his partiality for alcohol, which disrupted his career as a priest, and his relationships, often with married women, which led to duels and long feuds. Such self-stylization masks the story of an Enlightenment thinker willing to embrace the world; his inclination towards Freemasonry and his determination as a commoner to succeed in a world dominated by the aristocracy were characteristics which drove Casanova. The city that now proudly considers him amongst its greatest characters imprisoned him for his misdeeds, although this did not prevent his flight abroad.

THE HIGHLIGHTS: SAN MARCO

INFO Gondola trips

Campo San Moisè is dominated by the sumptuous façade of its eponymous church (below). Cross a bridge and enter the Via 22 Marzo with its elegant stores, a well-known shopping area (right). In Harry's Bar on the Calle Vallaresso you can refresh yourself with a classic Bellini cocktail (below right).

The best time for a gondola trip is early morning, when Venice's canals are still relatively clear and you get to see a bit more for your money; the costly fare during the day is even higher for a very short-seeming hour.
Central gondola stand: Campo San Moisè; Tel (041) 523 18 37.

The variety of Venetian life can be better observed in Campo San Moisè than almost anywhere else. Its east side is flanked by the eponymous church with its 17th-century baroque façade. Concealed within are the tombs of the Fini family and remarkable works of art, including the Tintoretto painting, *Washing of the Feet*. The Ca' Giustinian on the Grand Canal embodies the contrasting grandeur of temporal life. This late Gothic palace, once an exclusive hotel welcoming Marcel Proust and Giuseppe Verdi as guests, is now the administrative base of the Biennale. Places of leisure and pleasure lie between the two buildings: the Ridotto, a former casino, first became a playhouse and is now a hotel. The legendary Bellini, an aperitif made from prosecco and iced peach purée, was invented in Harry's Bar, as was a starter of raw steak, which was to become famous as *carpaccio*.

THE HIGHLIGHTS: SAN MARCO

Built to a design by Gianantonio Selva, the opera house was destroyed by fire in 1836 and rebuilt, burning down again in 1996. It has been reconstructed under the leadership of Aldo Rossi and reopened in 2004 (below). Right: Al Teatro restaurant near the opera house entrance.

INFO La Fenice

In addition to a tour (which is made easier with audio guides), the company also offers a guided tour conducted by an opera expert, with much interesting background information and an aperitif at the end.

Campo San Fantin; Tel (041) 78 66 74; box office 10.00–18.00, daily.

After Venice's most important opera house burned down in 1773, a new building was built between 1790 and 1792, receiving the name Gran Teatro La Fenice ("The Phoenix"), as it rose like a phoenix from the ashes. In the course of its history, in which two incarnations have burnt down, it has witnessed the world premieres of many important pieces: the first performances of Gioacchino Rossini's *Tancredi* and *Semiramide* took place in 1813 and 1823 respectively. In 1951 Igor Stravinsky's *The Rake's Progress* and in 1954 Benjamin Britten's *The Turn of the Screw* were first staged here. The original performances of Giuseppe Verdi's operas *Rigoletto* (1851) and *La Traviata* (1853) were particular highlights; the latter failed to please the audience, which nonetheless took the occasion as an opportunity to demand a separate Italian kingdom from their Habsburg rulers.

Venetian pride in its great musical tradition is to be found on every street corner (below). Below right: A portrait of Antonio Vivaldi by François Morellon de La Cave. Far right: A monument to Baldassare Galuppi (1706–1785) on the island of Burano; as a composer of over 100 operas, he was crucial to the development of opera *buffa* (comic opera). Right: A concert in the ballroom of the Ca' Rezzonico.

Venice has been a focus for innovative music since the middle of the 16th century. A group of composers known as the Venetian School charted the movement from Renaissance to baroque music. The Dutchman Adrian Willaert is considered their founder; further composers in this style, strengthening the position of polyphony in sacred music and championing instrumental music, were Cipriano de Rore, Claudio Merulo, Andrea and Giovanni Gabrieli, and the great Claudio Monteverdi, who died in Venice in 1643 at the age of 76, having brought opera to even greater heights. Venetian baroque music reaches its apotheosis in the works of Antonio Vivaldi (1678–1741). Born in the city as the son of a violinist and learning this instrument as a child, he initially preferred a career as a priest, later becoming a violin teacher and composer. Vivaldi is one of the few composers who was also known as a virtuoso performer. He created classics of the orchestral repertoire, such as *The Four Seasons*, and in particular shaped baroque music, with its violin solos and pieces in three movements. The illustrious Venetian gave over 300 concerts throughout Europe, although in his later years he was to experience a change in public taste towards the gallant musical style of the rococo period.

THE HIGHLIGHTS: SAN MARCO

INFO Guided tours

Right: The church, known by its Venetian name San Salvador, was given a baroque façade by Giuseppe Sardi. Below: Palazzo Contarini del Bovolo, with its striking stairwell, probably designed by Giorgio Spavento, is situated not far from Campo Manin.

Free guided tours are available to visitors to San Salvador. The tours, which take place at 16.00 every Wednesday from 2 May to 27 June, are available in Italian and English.

Campo San Salvador; Tel (041) 241 38 17; church opening times Mon–Sat 9.00–12.00, 15.00–18.00.

The three-naved Church of the Redeemer was constructed between 1507 and 1534 to a design in the Renaissance style by Giorgio Spavento and Tullio Lombardo; the façade is from the 17th century. The church's artistic jewel is Titian's 1566 masterpiece, *Annuncia-* *tion*, bringing to perfection his characteristic asymmetric picture composition. Another work here by the great painter is *Transfiguration of Christ* (1560). The nearby Palazzo Contarini del Bovolo received its current form in the 16th century when existing older buildings were altered. Pietro Contarini, whose extended family had provided no less than six doges, was responsible for the changes. The "palace of the snail shell", now home to the municipal waterworks, owes its name to the striking stairwell on the left side of the building.

The streets of the Mercerie represent Venice's main shopping district. In amongst the upmarket fashion boutiques, pastry shops, and delicatessens there are souvenir and antiques stores selling a variety of products. Carnival masks or puppets, velvet cushions, marbled paper, paintings, art deco lamps, lace from Burano, or glass from Murano; art and kitsch, exclusive products and real junk, are to be found next to one another in the little shops.

THE MERCERIE – SHOPPING PARADIS

The steps of many tourists, often female, slow on the way from the Torre del-l'Orologio to the Rialto Bridge; the store windows on the Mercerie would draw any gaze. Crafty merchants have traded in this maze of little streets since the earliest of times, perhaps giving rise to the name of the quarter, which translated means,

literally, "haberdashery". Far more than buttons and thread is on sale now, however – the traders' displays are piled with precious silks and satins, damask and brocades. Luxury boutiques selling clothes and leather goods have sought out the Mercerie, and famous names like Prada, Versace, Laura Biagiotti, Bulgari, and

Valentino will be known from elsewhere in the world. You have to hand it to the countless souvenir shops – nowhere else is the commercialization of the "myth of Venice" more apparent than here: the Carnival costumes, elaborate masks, Murano glass or Burano lace, and the variety of so-called antiques and

ornaments have practically nothing to do with Venetian tradition, but instead are aimed at the tastes of the masses, the tourists willing to pay. If you're not put off by all this costly kitsch, there are a few gems to be found, and if you have a sweet tooth you are at least in the right place to visit one of the many *pasticcerie*.

GRAND CANAL

The Grand Canal is Venice's main artery. Nearly 3,800 m (2.5 miles) long and lined with magnificent palaces, it almost always seems to be filled with gondolas, water taxis, and commercial boats, providing the city with everything it needs and even taking away the rubbish. It stretches in a long, lazy S-shape from the lagoon near Santa Lucia railway station to Saint Mark's Basin and is 30–90 m (98–295 feet) wide. The *vaporetto*, a sort of waterbus, is the vessel of choice for short journeys by public transport. Tourists are particularly fond of route No. 1, which goes from St Mark's Square to Piazzale Roma, permitting the leisurely inspection of many sights en route.

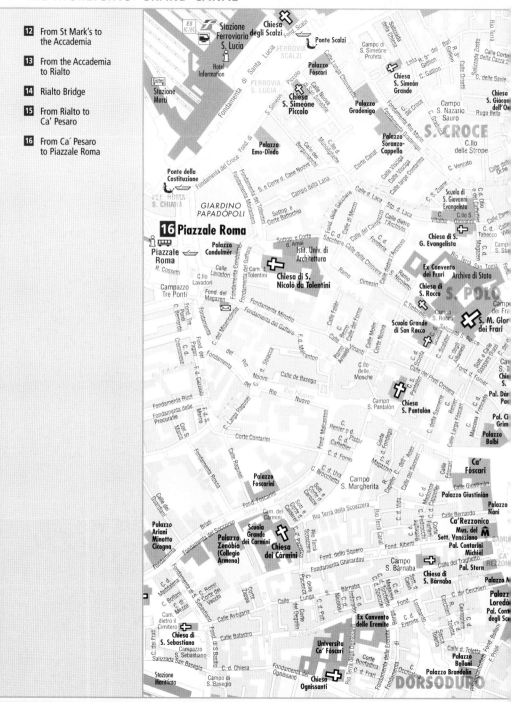

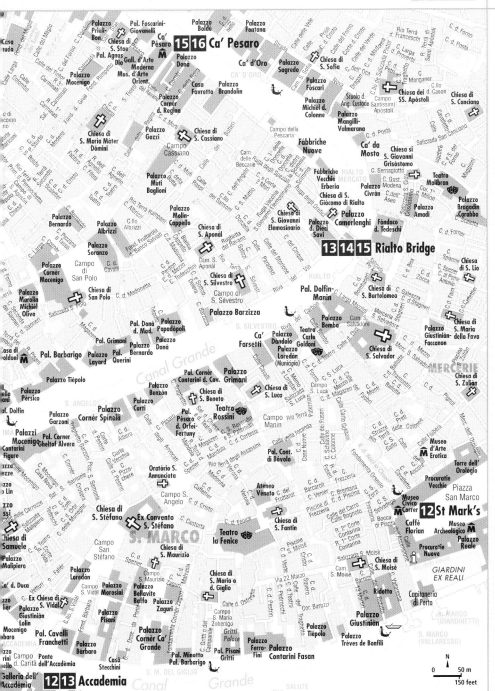

THE HIGHLIGHTS: GRAND CANAL

Right beside the Accademia Bridge, which gives a good view of the church of Santa Maria della Salute (right), is Palazzo Cavalli-Franchetti, a Gothic building with fine tracery (below). Below right: The late Gothic Palazzo Contarini Fasan has impressive arched windows and balconies with starfish-shaped ornamentation.

TIP Ai Gondolieri

This restaurant, which has bloomed from a workers' bar to one of the city's culinary jewels, is a stone's throw from the Accademia or Salute *vaporetto* stops.

Fondamenta Ospedalero; Tel (041) 528 63 96; Wed–Mon 12.00–15.30, 19.00–23.00.

If you go up the Grand Canal from St Mark's Square, you will soon see a building on the left side with a gold weather vane on top of it. Shaped like a ship's keel and once housing one of the most important authorities in Venice, the Dogana di Mare was the main customs house and is now a gallery for contemporary art. The white façade of Santa Maria della Salute is to be seen shining behind it, and opposite that is the 15th-century Palazzo Contarini Fasan, also known as the House of Desdemona, the Shakespearean heroine supposedly murdered here by her husband, Othello. One of the most expensive hotels in Venice, the Palazzo Gritti-Pisani, follows this on the right. Admire the marble Renaissance façade of Palazzo Dario, once an inspiration for the painter Claude Monet, who lived right in front of the modern, wooden Accademia Bridge in the magnificent Palazzo Barbaro.

THE HIGHLIGHTS: GRAND CANAL

INFO Palazzo Grassi

Palazzo Grassi (below) was completed by Giorgio Massari in 1772; Palazzo Cappello Malipiero Barnabò with its spectacular garden lies next to it (inset, below left). Massari's Ca' Rezzonico is a showcase for great art, including ceiling frescoes by Giovanni Battista Tiepolo (inset, below right).

The industrialist Pinault's art collection and the changing exhibitions attracts the crowds to this *palazzo*. Ticket reservations are especially recommended in the summer.

Campo San Samuele; Tel (041) 523 16 80; Wed–Mon 10.00–19.00, last admission 18.00.
www.palazzograssi.it

Palazzo Falier lies diagonally opposite the Accademia and was supposedly once inhabited by Doge Marin Falier, who was later beheaded for treason. On the left lies the baroque Ca' Rezzonico, built by Baldassare Longhena and Giorgio Massari, the home of the Museo del Settecento Veneziano, with frescoes by Giovanni Battista Tiepolo and an opulent ballroom with a trompe-l'œil ceiling fresco. Opposite this is another building by Massari, the early classical Palazzo Grassi, which is now used as an exhibition space. Further along to the right are three of the city's most important *palazzi*: Palazzo Mocenigo, built by combining four existing buildings, was once home to the English poet, Lord Byron; Palazzo Corner Spinelli, designed by Mauro Codussi, inspired many later Renaissance *palazzi*, as did Palazzo Grimani di San Luca with its three levels fronted by Corinthian columns.

TIP Bancogiro

Venice has more than 400 bridges, but the most famous is the Rialto Bridge (below), connecting the San Marco *sestiere* with the Rialto markets in San Polo. This limestone structure, completed in the 16th century, crosses the canal in a broad sweep and has room for two rows of shops (right).

The name of this *osteria* is derived from local history: one of Venice's first banks was based here. Nowadays, visitors can sample traditional Venetian cuisine and a superb selection of wines.
Campo San Giacometto; Tel (041) 523 20 61; Tues–Sun 10.30–15.00, 18.30–24.00 (except Sun evening).

Until the first Accademia Bridge was constructed in 1854, the only means of crossing the Grand Canal on foot was the Rialto Bridge. Lined with shops on both sides, this stone monument is a true symbol of Venice. Its central span, whose abutments rest on 12,000 tree trunks, describes a broad arch across the canal over a distance of 48 m (157 feet); its height of 7.5 m (25 feet) in the middle allows even large boats to pass. Its construction became necessary after a 13th-century wooden bridge on the site finally collapsed in 1444 under the weight of spectators watching the marriage procession of the Marchese di Ferrara. Another wooden structure was initially erected, although eventually a more solid solution was considered and finally constructed between 1588 and 1591 by Antonio da Ponte. The bridge has long defied da Ponte's critics, who thought the weight of the portico would bring it crashing into the canal.

Below: A boat trip on the Rio di San Lucca by Campo Manin. Building a genuine Venetian gondola is an elaborate procedure: nine different kinds of wood are used and 280 separate components must be fashioned and assembled. Gondolas are not only used for tourist trips on the canals, where traffic jams are common (below right), but also the gondola ferries – *traghetti* – cross the Grand Canal at points far from the bridges (right).

GONDOLAS, GONDOLIERS, TRAGHETT

Until the advent of the motorboat, gondolas ruled the waves on Venice's canals. Quite when this unique boat design was developed is now unclear, but they were certainly already known in the 11th century. In the High Middle Ages the gondolas were gaudily painted; black was not prescribed as the only permissible hue until 1562, to contrast with the excessive grandeur displayed by the water craft belonging to the influential nobility. A traditional gondola is about 11 m (36 feet) long and 1.5 m (5 feet) wide and steered only by a strap running over a forked rudder. To balance out the weight of the gondolier in the stern, the vehicle's bow is fitted with a so-called *fèrro*, a heavy metal covering. The gondolier's costume is as regulated as the construction of the boat: a striped shirt and black trousers finished off with a straw hat. Venice's gondoliers are known for not only their singing, which is intended to elicit a romantic mood in tourists expecting that sort of thing on their trip down the canals, but also for their steep prices, which are notorious. Visitors wishing to experience a gondola trip at rather more agreeable prices should take one of the *traghetti* – everyday gondolas, as it were – which serve as ferries across the Grand Canal.

THE HIGHLIGHTS: GRAND CANAL

TIP Osteria Ca' d'Oro

Below: The view from the Rialto Bridge at the bend in the Grand Canal, with Palazzo Camerlenghi on the left. The Ca' d'Oro (Golden House) is one of the city's most beautiful buildings and houses Titian's *Venus at the Mirror* (insets, below). The modern sculpture in the atrium is just one of the Ca' Pesaro's treasures (right).

This *osteria*, which is always busy, is known to locals as "alla Vedova", after a previous owner. Down-to-earth dishes are served on long tables in a convivial atmosphere.
Calle del Pistor; Tel (041) 528 53 24; 11.30–14.30, 18.30–22.30, daily (except Thurs and Sun lunchtime), closed in Aug.

Directly behind the Rialto Bridge and to the right lies the Fondaco dei Tedeschi, once occupied by German merchants and latterly the Venice headquarters for the Italian postal service. To the left is Palazzo Camerlenghi, which served as a residence for the city chamberlain and as a prison. The magnificent Gothic Ca' d'Oro, designed by Bartolomeo Bon, lies further up the canal to the right and houses the Galleria Franchetti with its Titian *Venus*, pieces from the workshops of Vittore Carpaccio, and Andrea Mantegna's moving *St Sebastian* (*c.* 1506). The three-floored Ca' Pesaro, a masterpiece of Venetian baroque, soon follows on the other side of the canal, and here the Galleria d'Arte Moderna is to be found, with works by Rodin, Chagall, and Klimt, amongst others. Ca' Pesaro is also home to the Museo d'Arte Orientale, one of the most significant collections of Chinese and Japanese art in Europe.

Hundreds of boats ply the Grand Canal every day. Below: A *vaporetto* stop. Below right, from top: More than 500 goods boats deliver about 850 tons of supplies daily, from provisions to building materials; the Venetians are not entirely keen on the cruise ships that visit the city, as here on the Riva degli Schiavoni – these can be up to 300 m (984 feet) long with massive propellers. Right: Even accidents and emergencies are dealt with by boat.

TRAFFIC IN VENICE

Think of Venice and you immediately picture people being transported along the canals in black gondolas, and these were indeed the city's main form of transport until the motorboat was developed. Things may have speeded up a bit since then, but things have not really changed a great deal; Venice's residents move around town in their own boats or use public transport – waterbuses called *vaporetti*. There are water taxis, water ambulances, and water hearses; goods, mail, and refuse are transported by water, and even the police and fire service are largely organized to use the canals, with the journey completed on foot from the quay. In other cities where there are streets, here there are canals. Wedding trains and funeral cortèges solemnly process along the Grand Canal, as do many religious processions. More than 50,000 commuters and over 30,000 tourists enter the city daily and board the *vaporetti*, which soon become crammed, with such bottlenecks as the Rialto Bridge descending into complete chaos. In addition to the logistical problems, the damage caused to the foundations of the *palazzi* by the wakes of motorboats is only exacerbated by the incongruous giant cruise ships that moor amid the Renaissance grandeur of the adjacent Giudecca Canal.

THE HIGHLIGHTS: GRAND CANAL

Constitution Bridge, a 94-m (308-foot) long steel and glass structure, connects the station and Piazzale Roma (below). Palazzo Labia's ballroom has astonishing frescoes by Tiepolo depicting scenes from the life of Cleopatra, including *The Meeting of Anthony and Cleopatra* (below right). Right: Fondaco dei Turchi.

TIP Rivetta

This typical *bacaro*, where locals meet to trade banter, drink wine from large, wicker-wrapped bottles, and eat a traditional snack of *cicchetti*, is to be found away from the tourist drags, near Santa Lucia station.
Calle Sechera; Mon–Sat 8.30–21.30, closed in Aug

Venice's casino is housed in the early Renaissance-style Palazzo Vendramin-Calergi, designed by Mauro Codussi; Richard Wagner died of a heart attack here in 1883, securing it a footnote in musical history. The Fondaco dei Turchi, a Byzantine-looking building once used as a warehouse by the Turks, lies opposite the casino and is home to the Natural History Museum. Palazzo Labia, with its opulent, late baroque ballroom designed by Giorgio Massari and with frescoes by Giovanni Battista Tiepolo, is located further up the canal. It has been used for gala events by the broadcaster RAI since 1964. Piazzale Roma is the last stop on the No. 1 *vaporetto* route, and here the highest and longest bridge over the Grand Canal has been built out of steel and glass by a Spanish architect, Santiago Calatrava; the slender Constitution Bridge was opened in 2008. It offers a panoramic view over the Grand Canal.

The western suburbs of Santa Croce and San Polo were amongst the first areas of Venice to be settled. This high point of the lagoon, called the Rivo Alto, the "high shore", was safe from flooding and had become the site of the Rialto markets. Trade in fresh food, especially fish, is still a part of life in this suburb, which is as lively as it is steeped in tradition. There are all kinds of little stores and workshops, enchanting cafés and *osterie*, which lend atmosphere to the alleyways and squares. The historical art highlights are the Gothic Frari church and the Scuola Grande di San Rocco.

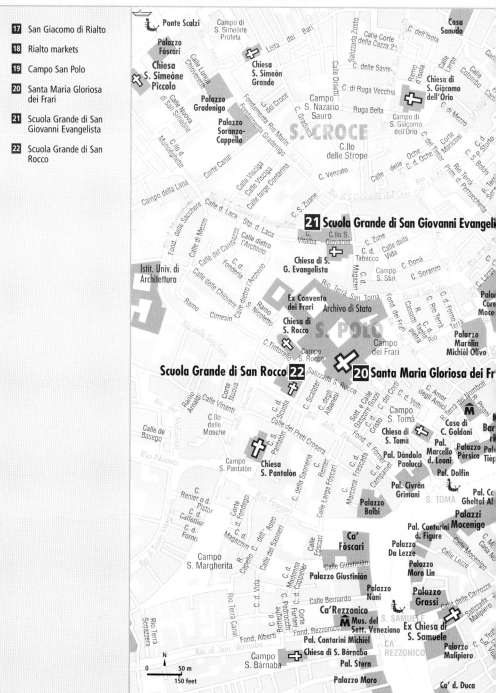

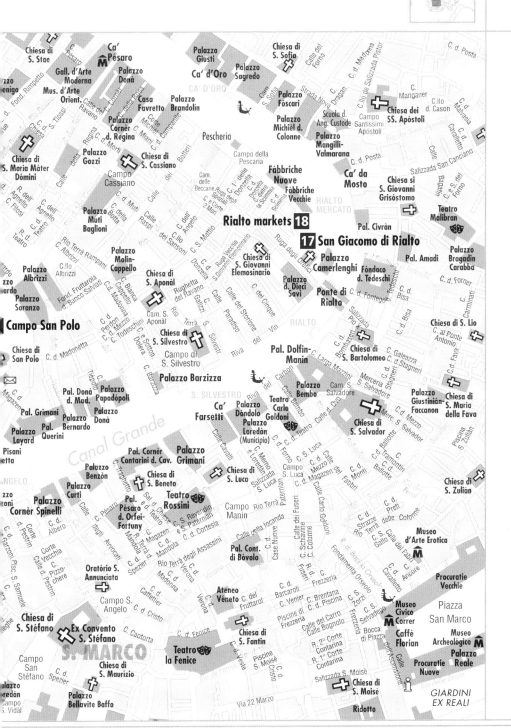

THE HIGHLIGHTS: SANTA CROCE AND SAN POLO

Fish and shellfish are sold in the Pescheria (below), built in 1907. Fruit and veg from the mainland and the market garden islands are brought to market by boat. Merchants once used to conduct business in front of the church of San Giacomo di Rialto (right), which lies to the west of the Erberia.

TIP Trattoria alla Madonna

This *trattoria* is considered an institution – practically nowhere else can you find such a selection of fresh fish. State visitors are often brought to dine here.

Calle della Madonna/Calle dei Cinque; Tel (041) 522 38 24; Thurs–Tues 12.00–15.00, 19.00–22.30.

San Giacamo di Rialto, Venice's oldest church with a history dating back to the 5th century, lies between the Rialto Bridge and the Rialto markets. Refurbished in the 17th century, its most striking feature is a large Gothic clock. A statue from 1540 of Gobbo, the hunchback, stands to the left of San Giacomo; this hunched figure supports a step from which laws and court sentences were once proclaimed, and which also marked the end of "running the gauntlet" – a punishment in which miscreants had to scramble here from St Mark's whilst being beaten with sticks. The markets are always lively: the Pescheria sells fish and seafood, the Erberia fruit, vegetables, and herbs. Both gourmets and browsers are attracted in equal numbers, attracting numerous and adept pickpockets.

THE HIGHLIGHTS:
SANTA CROCE
AND SAN POLO

TIP All'Arco

The square is named after the church of San Polo (below), in whose interior great works of art are to be found, such as Tintoretto's *Last Supper* (right). The square was once the scene of not only great processions but also bear- and bull-baiting, as depicted in this 1648 painting by Joseph Heintz the Younger (inset, below).

At lunchtimes, even the standing places are filled in this popular *osteria*. After shopping in the market, Venice meets up here for a glass of wine and a few of the snacks arranged appetizingly along the bar. *Rialto, Calle dell'Occhialer; Tel (041) 520 56 66; Mon–Sat 8.00–16.00.*

Campo San Polo is of great importance to the city's history, indeed of an importance reaching beyond Venice: Lorenzino de' Medici, who had previously murdered his cousin Alessandro in the struggle for power over Tuscan Florence, was stabbed to death here in 1548. Venice's second-largest square is flanked to the west by the Gothic church of San Polo, whose origins date back to the 9th century. Inside, there are impressive baroque crucifixion scenes in the oratory, completed by the painter Giovanni Domenico Tiepolo in 1749. His father, Giovanni Battista, created a painting for the north aisle. Palazzo Soranzo, to the east of the square, was constructed by combining two older buildings, and next door is Palazzo Maffetti Tiepolo, designed by Domenico Rossi. The land entrance to Palazzo Corner Mocenigo is to be found in its enchanting façade in the north-west corner of the square.

The *palazzo* in which Goldoni first saw the light of day has a feature typical of Venetian Gothic – narrow, high windows with pointed arches (below). The author's statue stands in Campo Bartolomeo, near the Rialto Bridge (below right). Right: The baroque resplendence of the Ca' Goldoni is to be found at Campo San Luca.

CARLO GOLDONI AND THE CA' GOLDONI

Venice's greatest baroque writer was Carlo Goldoni (1707–1793), who sought to redefine Italian comedy, a genre that had been much influenced by the traditions of the Commedia dell'Arte. Born in Venice, he wrote some 200 plays in the Venetian dialect which bound the actors much more strictly to the script, creating socio-critical, character-based comedies in the tradition of Molière, free from improvised scenes. Such successful works as *The Servant of Two Masters* (1745) and *Mirandolo* (1752) feature to this day in the repertoire of drama companies throughout the world. Goldoni, a qualified lawyer who for many years was obliged by financial worries to work as an advocate, was also a librettist. He wrote about 80 mostly three-act plays in *opera buffa* form, which he described as *dramma gio-coso* (literally "jocular drama"). His birthplace, not far from the southern bank of the Grand Canal, houses a communal study organization for the history of the-ater, with a library and a memorial room dedicated to the great poet. With its 15th-century interior court-yard housing a stone stair-well that is well worth seeing, this late Gothic *palazzo* has a rather special atmosphere, which is none too surprising given the his-torical importance of its for-mer inhabitant.

This Franciscan church is one of Venice's most important religious buildings. Below: A view from the central aisle to the high altar and Titian's *Assumption of the Virgin* (below right). The sacristy houses an early Renaissance masterpiece in Giovanni Bellini's *Madonna and Child with Saints* (right).

INFO Church concerts

The Frari's two restored 18th-century organs are often featured in exquisite concerts lent all the more distinction by appearances by internationally esteemed performers.

Campo dei Frari; Tel (041) 272 86 11. Concert information: www.basilicadeifrari.it

Construction of this Gothic church, known as the Frari for short, was begun by the mendicant Franciscan order in 1340 as a three-aisled pillar basilica with a high transept, six small and one large choir chapels, and an adjoining cloister on the site of a previous building. Its hall-like interior and Gothic ribbed ceiling direct the eye to an almost 7-m (23-foot) tall rood screen, decorated with sculptures of saints by Bartolomeo Bon and Pietro Lombardo, behind which are concealed some magnificent choir stalls. Of its many outstanding works of art, two altarpieces by Titian and a statue of St John by Donatello are especially worthy of mention. Many great Italian personalities are buried in the Frari and there are many strikingly beautiful tombs, including those of the doges Nicolò Tron and Francesco Foscari, the sculptor Canova, and the great master Titian himself.

Titian's painting technique was a great influence on Western art from the 17th to the 20th centuries (below right: *Self Portrait*, *c.* 1567, in the Prado in Madrid). *The Presentation of the Virgin Mary at the Temple* was painted between 1534 and 1538 for the Scuola Santa Maria della Carità (right). *The Annunciation,* completed in 1543 for the Scuola Grande di San Rocco, is vivid and yet delicate (below).

TITIAN

The artist Titian is considered to be the epitome of Italian High Renaissance painting. Tiziano Vecellio (c. 1488–1576) was trained in Italy – allegedly by Giorgione – and spent the greater part of his life in the country. His typically sensitive use of color, incorporation of space and light, and the vivacity of his motifs seem to anticipate the baroque and are already perceptible in his two early masterpieces for Santa Maria Gloriosa dei Frari: the magnificent altarpiece, *Assumption of the Virgin* (1516–18), and the *Pesaro Madonna* (1519– 26). Titian first painted the emperor Charles V in 1533, becoming his official court painter and accepting a title; some 12 years later he created a likeness of Pope Paul III and began his famous *Neapolitan Danae*. In 1550 he was commissioned to paint King Philip II of Spain, for whom he also created the *Poesie* series of paintings. During the last years of his life Titian returned to Venice and created a late masterpiece in the crepuscular *Martyrdom of St Lawrence* for the Jesuit Church, before finally falling victim to a plague epidemic. Titian's late work is distinguished by a renewed freshness and spiritual refinement, as instanced in the *Pietà* (displayed in the Accademia), which he painted for his own tomb.

THE HIGHLIGHTS: SANTA CROCE AND SAN POLO

INFO Great opera

The *scuola*'s courtyard, designed by Pietro Lombardo, is a Renaissance masterpiece (below). The main hall was constructed between 1727 and 1762 (below right). In 1581, Palma Il Giovane painted four pictures for the Sala dell'Albergo, including an apocalyptic picture of the seven-headed beast (right).

The main hall is used several times a month to stage masterpieces of Italian opera, including works by Puccini, Verdi, and Rossini. The rooms are otherwise only viewable by making an appointment in advance by telephone.
Campiello San Giovanni; Tel (041) 71 82 34. www.scuolasangiovanni.it

The so-called scuola ("schools") were institutions founded by lay brotherhoods to serve religious and charitable purposes, as well as to increase the prestige of the confraternity. In 1480, Pietro Lombardo designed a geometric portal of strict proportions (as indebted to Renaissance ideals as Mauro Codussi's later magnificent double staircase of 1498) for the school founded by the Confraternity of St John the Evangelist, whose most valuable possession was a supposed relic of the True Cross. Although the *scuola*'s most important artworks – a 16th-century series of pictures by Venetian artists inspired by the relic – now grace the walls of the Accademia, its interior is still well worth seeing, even if it is a little off the usual tourist trail, thanks to paintings and frescoes by Tintoretto, Palma Il Giovane, and Tiepolo, not to mention a large collection of valuable Gothic sacred art.

THE HIGHLIGHTS:
SANTA CROCE
AND SAN POLO

INFO San Rocco Church

The elaborate Renaissance façade of the *scuola* (below) is a clue to the importance of the confraternity. Tintoretto created a magnificent picture cycle for the *scuola*, of which his 1567 painting of *Christ before Pilate*, now in the Sala dell'Albergo, once formed a part (below right). Right: The Upper Hall.

There are four further masterpieces by Tintoretto in the church of San Rocco, including startling depictions of the plague epidemic in Venice.

Campo San Rocco; Tel (041) 523 48 64; summer 8.00–12.30, 15.00–17.00, daily, winter Mon–Fri 8.00–12.30, 15.00–17.00, Sat, Sun 8.00–12.30.

The most magnificent of Venice's great *scuole* is dedicated to St Roch, the patron saint of plague and epidemic victims. Construction of the Scuola Grande di San Rocco was begun by Bartolomeo Bon in 1517 and completed in a Renaissance style in 1549 by Scarpagnino, a master whose work is also to be seen in the enormous staircase. Tintoretto was commissioned to decorate the building's interior in 1564, and over the course of the next 23 years he created 56 monumental wall and ceiling paintings. Amongst his masterpieces are scenes from the Old and New Testaments on the upper floor, and in particular a series of paintings on the ground floor illustrating the life of the Madonna and a Crucifixion in the Sala dell'Albergo. In these, the painter has perfected his characteristic representation of religious sensibility through the depiction of a living figure in a landscape flooded with light.

DORSODURO, LA GIUDECCA, AND SAN GIORGIO MAGGIORE

PONTE
PUG

Rich in tradition, the district of Dorsoduro, with its outlying, sickle-shaped island La Giudecca and the small monastery island of San Giorgio, lies to the south of Venice. Dorsoduro literally means "hard back", an indication of the rocky ground on which this quarter is built. Originally inhabited by fishermen, since the Middle Ages the Dorsduro has developed into a sort of architecture park, boasting magnificent palaces on the Grand Canal and countless important church buildings. At heart, however, this district still belongs to the people, and the modern atmosphere is if anything close-knit.

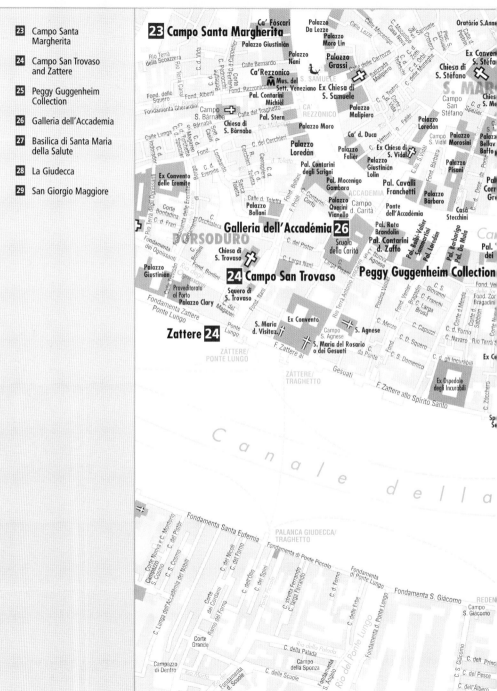

Ateneo
Véneto
C. d.
Fruttarol
C. d. Barcaroli
C. Venier
C. Brentana
C. d. Piscina
Piscine di
Frezzeria
Frezzeria
Frezzeria
Orseolo
C. Cavaletto
Procuratie
Vecchie
Piazza
San Marco

**Basilica di
San Marco**

**Mus. Diocesano
d'Arte Sacra**
Corte
Solastica
Campo
S. Zaccaria

Chiesa di
S. Fantin
C. d. Carro
Caffe Bognolo
Museo
Civico Correr

Campanile
Loggetta
Ponte dei
Sospiri
Palazzo
Dándolo
C. d. Vin

Teatro
la Fenice
C. d. Fenice
Piscine di
S. Moisé
Bocca
di Piazza
Caffè
Florian
Museo
Archeológico

Palazzo
Ducale
Palazzo
d. Prigioni
Riva degli Schiavoni

Chiesa di
S. Maria o
d. Giglio
Salizzada S. Moisé
Cam.
S. Moisé
Chiesa di
S. Moisé
Procuratie
Nuove
Palazzo
Reale
Palazzo
Zecca
Libreria
Sansoviniana
Piazzetta
San
Marco
Molo

PAGLIA
S. ZACCARIA
(DANIELI)
S. ZACCARIA
(JOLANDA)

Campo
S. Maria
Zobenigo
Gritti
Palace
Via 22 Marzo
C. d. Teatro
Cor. Barozzi
Ridotto
GIARDINI
EX REALI
Capitaneria
di Porto

S. MARCO
(GIARDINETTI)

Pal. Pisani
Gritti
Palazzo
Ferro-
Fini
Palazzo
Tiépolo
Palazzo
Giustiniàn
Palazzo
Tréves de Bonfili

S. MARCO
(VALLARESSO)

Palazzo
Contarini Fasan

Canale di San Marco

Grande
SALUTE
Fondamenta della Dogana alla Salute
Canale di San Marco

Palazzo
Genovese
Ex Abbazia di
S. Gregorio
Campo della
Salute
Semin.
Patriarc.
Dogana
da Mar

27 Basílica di Santa Maria della Salute

Ex Chiesa di
S. Gregório
Rio Terrà
del Catecúmeni

Ex Ospedale
d. Catecúmeni

Campo
S. Giórgio
S. GIORGIO

San Giorgio Maggiore 29

Saloni
Ex Magazzini
del Sale
Fondazione
Cini

Giudecca

Campo
Nani e Bárbaro
Fondamenta S. Giovanni

Canale di San Giorgio

*Isola della
Giudecca*

ZITELLE
Fondamenta delle Zitelle
Chiesa delle
Zitelle
Ex Convento

**QUARTIERE CAMPO
DI MARTE**

Fondamenta della Croce
C. Rio la Croce
C. Michelángelo
C. dell'Asilo Masón
C. 3° Campalto
C. 4° Campalto

Ex Chiesa
della Croce
C. del Gran
Campiello
Campalto
Campiello
Ospizio

28 La Giudecca
C. larga Grani
C. Esterna
C. larga
della Cooperativa

N

0   100 m
300 feet

THE HIGHLIGHTS:
DORSODURO,
LA GIUDECCA, AND
SAN GIORGIO MAGGIORE

TIP Nightlife

Dorsoduro's largest square is crammed with market stalls piled high with fish, fruit, and vegetables, small stores, cafés, and restaurants. It is little wonder that bars such as Caffé Rosso are always full (below). Right: The magnificent main hall of the Scuola Grande dei Carmini.

Dorsoduro's main square is not just thronged during the day – a bustling night life has developed here over the last few years. There are any number of bars, pubs, music venues, and cabaret stages offering lively, atmospheric entertainment.

This lengthy square owes its name to the church of Santa Margherita on its northern side, whose interior conceals a ceiling fresco by Constantino Cedini; once a church, it is now the main hall of the university. Of the buildings lining the lively market in the square, two are of particular note: the first, the Scuola dei Varotari was built for the confraternity of tanners in the first half of the 18th century and it stands alone in the middle of the square. Behind the Scuola dei Varotari, in the southern corner of the square, stands the Carmelite church of Santa Maria, whose treasures include Cima da Conegliano's *Adoration of the Shepherds* (*c.* 1509) and Lorenzo Lotto's *St Nicholas* (*c.* 1529). The adjoining 17th-century Scuola Grande dei Carmini has an enchanting ballroom, with beautiful ceiling frescoes created by the great Giovanni Battista Tiepolo in 1740.

THE HIGHLIGHTS: DORSODURO, LA GIUDECCA, AND SAN GIORGIO MAGGIORE

INFO Gondola workshop

Not far from Campo San Trovaso lie the charms of Cantine del Vino on the Ponte San Trovaso, a typical Venetian bar with standing room only, which serves wine and culinary delicacies (below). Below right, from top: Squero di San Trovaso – centuries of traditional gondola manufacture. Right: The Zattere, a charming canalside promenade.

Squero di San Trovaso, on the square of the same name, is one of the last active gondola workshops. The actual workshop is closed to the public, but the gondola builders can be watched at work from the opposite side of the canal.
Campo San Trovaso (Fondamenta Bontini); Tel (041) 522 91 46.

CAMPO SAN TROVASO AND ZATTERE **24**

The 16th-century Chiesa dei Santi Gervasio e Protasio, known universally as San Trovaso, lends its name to this square. Quite who created the beautiful marble reliefs in the Clary chapel is uncertain, but there are also two works by Tintoretto and paintings by Palma Il Giovane and Giuseppe Ponga. The canal side opposite the church has a view of the Squero di San Trovaso, one of the few remaining workshops still building gondolas in the traditional manner. You might even be tempted to spend some time in one of the cafés on the Zattere, the long broad quay alongside the nearby Canal della Giudecca, which has become a popular location for a stroll and is also where the church of Santa Maria del Rosario is to be found. Known as Gesuati for short, the church houses magnificent ceiling frescoes and a picture of the Madonna painted by Giovanni Battista Tiepolo in 1738.

THE HIGHLIGHTS:
DORSODURO, LA GIUDECCA, AND SAN GIORGIO MAGGIORE

TIP Museum Café

The art enthusiast Peggy Guggenheim amassed one of the world's most important private collections of modern painting and sculpture in her home. Below right: Equestrian sculpture by Marino Marini. Right: The great collector at home, the 18th-century Palazzo Venier dei Leoni.

The chefs of the Osteria ai Gondolieri are also responsible for the Guggenheim café and its famously excellent cuisine. The superb view of the sculpture garden in the round is an additional pleasure.
Palazzo Venier dei Leoni, Dosoduro 704; Tel (041) 240 54 11; Wed–Mon 10.00–18.00.

Viewed from the Grand Canal, Palazzo Venier dei Leoni looks like a bungalow. Originally intended to be laid out on several floors, the building was purchased by the American millionairess Peggy Guggenheim and never completed beyond the ground floor. This rather eccentric lady lived here for 30 years and lies buried in the garden, next to her beloved dogs. The works she brought together, augmented in no small way with Biennale purchases, represent one of the greatest collections in the art world. There are paintings by Guggenheim's second husband, Max Ernst, and by her protégé Jackson Pollock, not to mention any number of other outstanding 20th-century artists. Marino Marini's bronze, *The Angel of the City* (1948), certainly catches the eye; when religious processions were likely to stray too close to the *palazzo*, the figure's erect penis used to be carefully unscrewed (see p. 186).

Sacred motifs in a worldly city: Gentile Bellini's *The Miracle of the Cross on San Lorenzo Bridge* (below). Below right, from top: *Madonna and Child with Saints* by Antonio Vivarini and Giovanni d'Alemagna; Vittore Carpaccio's *The Ambassadors Return to the English Court*; Paolo Veronese's *Feast in the House of Levi*.

TIP Agli Alboretti

In 1750 the great Venetian painter Giovanni Battista Piazzetta initiated the founding of the Accademia, whose art holdings are principally the result of the dissolution of Venice's churches and monasteries in Napoleon's time. Because of this, the Accademia was able to occupy the vacant church of Santa Maria della Carità and its *scuola*, and then expand into the dissolved monastery of the Lateran Canons. There are important works by pretty much every Venetian master painter from the early Middle Ages to the rococo period to be found here, and particular attractions include Giorgione's fairytale painting *The Tempest* (c. 1507), Paolo Veneziano's polyptych *Coronation of the Virgin* (c. 1350), Paolo Veronese's *Feast in the House of Levi* (1573), which once caused religious controversy, and Vittore Carpaccio's eight-part cycle of paintings depicting *Stories from the Life of St Ursula* (1490–1500) (see p. 180).

Venice was always a hothouse of artistic creativity of the first order: in 1345 Paolo Veneziano created the wooden frame for the Pala d'Oro altarpiece in St Mark's (right). Below left, clockwise: Giorgione, *The Tempest* (c. 1507); Tintoretto, *Paradise*, (1588); Giovanni Domenico Tiepolo, *Pulcinella and the Acrobats* (c. 1793); Titian, *Pietà* (1576). Below right, clockwise: Canaletto, *Entrance to the Grand Canal* (1730); Giovanni Bellini, *Mary with the Boy Jesus, Standing Giving a Blessing* (c. 1470); Pietro Longhi, *Rhinoceros* (1751).

LIGHT AND SHADE – VENETIAN PAINTING

Venetian painting is famous for its glowing colors and shimmering light effects. Stylized early medieval Byzantine figuration was retained here longer than elsewhere and it was not until the first half of the 14th century that Veneziano attempted a synthesis of elements of Byzantine and Gothic styles. Andrea Mantegna's pictures of the Bellini family in the early Renaissance emphasized space and the physicality of form. The rise of the new technique of oil painting exerted great influence on choice of colors, and Vittore Carpaccio's narrative skill and the gentle light of Giorgione's world were augmented by the emotion and rich contrast found in Titian, whose works can hardly be bettered, at least in the High Renaissance. Painters active in 16th-century Venice, such as Tintoretto, Palma Il Giovane, and Paolo Veronese, cleared the way for the dynamic movement and control of light of baroque art, resulting in the almost excessive sumptuousness of the rococo period as seen in the works of Tiepolo, both junior and senior. Venetian art reached its apotheosis in the 18th century in masters such as Canaletto and Guardi, just as Rosalba Carriera was gaining popularity as a portrait artist and Pietro Longhi's genre paintings were ironically reflecting Venetian society.

THE HIGHLIGHTS: DORSODURO, LA GIUDECCA, AND SAN GIORGIO MAGGIORE

In contrast to the rather pompous exterior, the interior of this baroque church at the entrance to the Grand Canal is surprisingly light and architecturally restrained. Below right, from top: The statuary group on the high altar, created by Josse de Corte; *The Marriage at Cana*, a masterpiece by Tintoretto, hangs in the sacristy.

INFO Organ recitals

The1782 Dacci organ can be heard during Mass on Mondays to Fridays at 16.00 and on Sundays at 11.00. Musically exquisite vesper services are held every Saturday at 16.00.

Campo della Salute; Tel (041) 241 10 18; church opening times 9.00–12.00, 15.00–17.30, daily.

A baroque basilica constructed at the confluence of the Grand Canal and the Canale di San Marco, the Basilica di Santa Maria della Salute was dedicated to St Mary of Salvation in thanks for the ending of a plague epidemic in 1630. Works were begun by Baldassare Longhena, but not completed until 1692, five years after his death. The octagonal core building with its large cupola and characteristic giant volutes is supported by thousands of tree trunks. The sacristy is a treasure trove of Venetian painting, with Tintoretto's *Marriage at Cana*, signed in 1561, and three great ceiling paintings created by Titian between 1540 and 1549: *Cain and Abel*, *Abraham and Isaac*, and *David and Goliath*. Another of his paintings, *St Mark Enthroned with Saints Cosmas, Damian, Sebastian, and Roch* (1511–12) was commissioned for the church of Santo Spirito either during or just after an outbreak of the plague.

THE HIGHLIGHTS: DORSODURO, LA GIUDECCA, AND SAN GIORGIO MAGGIORE

INFO Festa del Redentore

The church, Il Redentore, built in thanks for surviving the plague, is one of the highlights of La Giudecca (below); its name is remembered in a procession. Below right, from top: the Molino Stucky; a rural idyll on the island; and the Crea gondola workshop.

One of Venice's most beautiful festivals takes place on the third Sunday in July. A pontoon bridge is built across the Giudecca Canal for the Festa del Redentore, and fireworks and light shows lend brilliance to the celebrations. Hundreds of illuminated boats ply the canals from the night preceding the event.

Thanks to its fish-skeleton shape, the Giudecca island group lying across from the Dorsoduro *sestiere* was once known as Spinalunga ("long spine"). Once the preserve of patrician homes, all Venetians now aspire to live here. Lying in the west of the island, the Molino Stucky, a neo-Gothic former flour mill and pasta factory complex built at the end of the 19th century by the German architect Ernst Wullekopf, was once the largest of its kind in Italy and is now a five-star hotel. The church of Il Redentore, whose construction was led by the great Andrea Palladio between 1577 and 1592, is to be found in the middle of the island. Topped with a great dome, this votive church consecrated in thanks for the end of a plague epidemic has a marble façade recalling classical temple structures. The pediment is topped with a statue of Christ the Redeemer (Redentore) bearing the cross.

THE HIGHLIGHTS: DORSODURO, LA GIUDECCA, AND SAN GIORGIO MAGGIORE

INFO Panorama

The modern complex of buildings, with a church façade designed to be viewed from afar, shows Palladian influences (below). The monastery and island are owned by the Giorgio Cini Foundation and used as a cultural center. Inset, below: *The Last Supper* of 1594 was one of Tintoretto's last works.

The Palladian campanile of the monastery offers a spectacular view of the entire city. A monk in an elevator awaits visitors at the end of the nave.
Isola San Giorgio Maggiore; Tel (041) 522 78 27; 9.30–12.30, 14.30–18.30 (16.30 in winter), daily.

There is a wonderful view from the Piazzetta across the Canale di San Marco to the brilliant-white marble façade of the church of San Giorgio Maggiore, located on its eponymous island. A three-naved Benedictine church designed by Andrea Palladio in 1565 with a floor plan based on a Latin cross, the church's long monks' choir and campanile were completed only after the architect's death. The monastery building and cloisters were also constructed according to his plans. The classical Roman influence is unmistakable, especially in the church's light interior. Baldassare Longhena's tomb for Procurator Lorenzo Venier (1667) and Girolama Campagna's high altar are worthy of particular attention. Two of the great paintings located in the presbytery, *The Miracle of Manna* and *The Last Supper*, are late masterpieces from Tintoretto's mature period.

THE HIGHLIGHTS

CANNAREGIO

At one time sparsely populated and covered in thick sedge (*canna*), Cannaregio is now Venice's northernmost district. The city's Jews were banished here in the 15th century, and it was these initially unprepossessing surroundings that were first called a ghetto. Nowadays, Cannaregio is the most densely populated area of the city and a base for a variety of light industry, a situation brought about by its location on the Grand Canal, which forms the district's southern border, and the construction of the Santa Lucia railway station in the 19th century, which helped the town to grow.

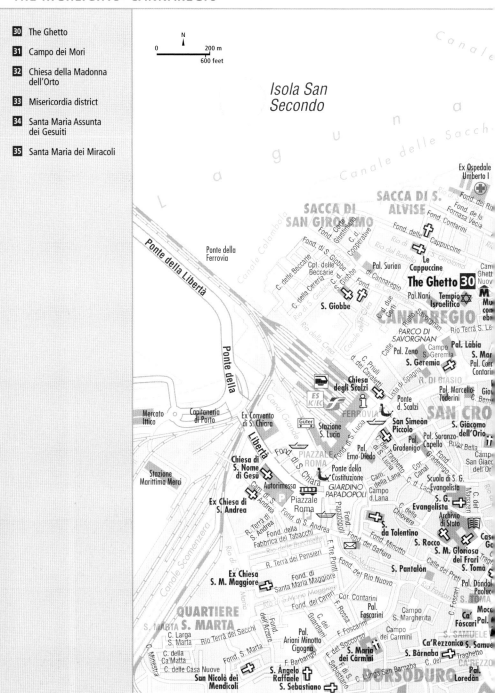

THE HIGHLIGHTS: CANNAREGIO

INFO Guided tours

Campo del Ghetto Nuovo was once the hub of the Jewish population's segregated district (below). As it was forbidden to build synagogues on Venetian soil, they were often built on the roofs (below right). The Scuola Spagnola is Venice's largest synagogue (right).

The guided tour of the synagogues, in English from the Museo Ebraico, provides background information on Jewish life in Venice.

Campo del Ghetto Nuovo, Cannaregio 2902/b; Tel (041) 71 53 59; from 10.30, then hourly, daily; last tour 17.30 (1 Jun–30 Sept), 15.30 (1 Oct–31 May).

In general, a ghetto was a restricted area of a medieval city within which Jews were allowed to live, excluded from the Christian community. Venice's original ghetto is to be found in Cannaregio, the area to which the Council of Ten banished the city's Jews in an edict of 1516. The settlement owes its name to a foundry (*geto*) that had previously occupied the site. Although the old ghetto was expanded into the Ghetto Nuovo in 1633, constraints of space still meant that the buildings here were constructed considerably higher than in other areas of Venice. Since the persecution and oppression of the German occupation in the 20th century, there are practically no Jews left living in Cannaregio. Only the Museo Ebraico and several synagogues (the museum organizes tours of them) recall the district's Jewish history, and there are a few restaurants and stores selling Jewish produce.

THE HIGHLIGHTS: CANNAREGIO

The four statues on the Campo dei Mori are possibly of Arabic origin and date from the 14th century (below). The painter Jacopo Robusti lived on the square, receiving the nickname Il Tintoretto ("the little dyer") because of his father's profession. Right: Tintoretto's house and a self-portrait.

TIP Anice Stellato

Famous for its excellent fish dishes, this hidden-away *osteria* is pleasantly quiet even in high season. The daily specials on its menu are definitely worth trying.

Fondamenta della Sensa; Tel (041) 72 07 44; Wed–Sun 12.30–14.00, 19.30–22.00 until end of Aug

Campo dei Mori owes its name to four Arabic-looking statues situated in niches set into houses on the square. These venerable relics of the high Middle Ages supposedly represent the three Mastelli brothers, merchants belonging to a family from the Peloponnese who built their *palazzo* beside the Rio Madonna dell'Orto in the 12th century. The statue of Antonio Rioba Mastelli was later fitted with an iron nose into which people would place satirical verse and even seditious tracts. The fourth statue, the figure of a merchant with an outsize turban, is to be found at 3399, Fondamenta dei Mori, a house whose crumbling condition would never lead you to suspect that it once belonged to Tintoretto. The great painter, commemorated in a Latin inscription on a plaque affixed to the building, lived here with his family from 1574 until his death on 31 May 1594.

THE HIGHLIGHTS: CANNAREGIO

INFO Secret tip

Somewhat hidden away, this church with its late Gothic brick façade is one of the most beautiful in the city (below right). Amongst its statuary is this Virgin of Mercy (right). One of the most impressive features of the interior is Tintoretto's painting, *The Worship of the Golden Calf* (below).

The area around the church is one of the most peaceful and romantic in Venice, and there are still little gardens to be found everywhere here. The square in front of the church with its view of the canal is a real oasis of peace.

Translated literally, this church is known as "the Holy Mother of the Vegetable Patch". The name refers to a statue of St Mary, reputed to work miracles, that was found in a local garden and is now installed in the church itself, in the Cappella San Mauro. Built in Campo dei Mori in the 14th century, the church's six bays were reconstructed in a late Gothic style in the 15th century. The tombs of Jacopo Tintoretto and his son, Domenico, can be found here. Tintoretto painted a series of pictures for the church between 1562 and 1564, including *The Last Judgment* and *The Worship of the Golden Calf*, which are displayed in the choir. Cima da Conegliano's *St John the Baptist and Saints* (*c.* 1493) is also worth searching out. An altarpiece painted by Giovanni Bellini in 1478 was stolen from the church in 1993. It was supposedly commissioned by Luca Navagero for his tomb elsewhere in the church.

The best way to experience Venetian cuisine is to sit outside an *osteria* or *trattoria*, as here, by the Fondamenta della Misericordia (below). Snacks called *cicchetti* (right) are very popular and are enjoyed with a glass of wine. A spritzer is a popular Venetian aperitif and is recommended to start an evening out.

OMBRA E CICCHETTI – VENETIAN CUISINE

In Venice, *ombra e cicchetti* is synonymous with good living. An *ombra* is a quick, refreshing 10 cl (3.5 fl oz) glass of chilled white wine or prosecco, to be found on every corner of the city in standing cafés called *bacari*, and *cicchetti* are the canapés served with it, little morsels of meat or seafood with a garnish to spice them up. Even these snacks are a clue to the variety for which Venetian cuisine has been famous for centuries. Constant deliveries of produce and truffles from the fertile Veneto and supplies of rare spices and recipes brought in by sea traders have combined and evolved into a cuisine around the lagoon that even in the 17th century was considered exceptional, featuring just the variety of seafood and fish one might expect from a mighty marine power. The most popular dishes utilize base ingredients such as mussels, octopus, crab, monkfish, and Dover sole, and serve them with vegetables and rice or polenta. As a starter, the chef might serve a dish invented in Harry's Bar, an establishment in Venice that has gone down in literary history: *carpaccio*, raw beef mince with vinaigrette. *Tiramisù* is a popular pudding. This rich dessert is full of cholesterol and was supposedly invented in Venetian courtesans for their exhausted men – the name means "pick me up"!

THE HIGHLIGHTS: CANNAREGIO

TIP Vini da Gigio

A stroll along the Rio della Misericordia gives a real impression of normal Venetian life (below). Below right: A *palazzo* on the Canale della Misericordia. Right, from left: The façade of the church of Santa Maria della Misericordia next to the Scuola Vecchia; a relief Madonna.

The choice of wine at Paolo Lazzari's *osteria* is famed far and wide; the best course is to follow the manager's recommendations. Even locals are attracted by the excellent Venetian cuisine.
Fondamenta di San Felice; Tel (041) 528 51 40; Wed–Sun 12.15–15.00, 19.30–22.00.

This district, named after the church of Santa Maria della Misericordia and its attendant *scuola*, lies to the east of the Chiesa della Madonna dell'Orto. The older *scuola* building was erected in the 14th century and is still Gothic in style; the Scuola Nuova was designed by Jacopo Sansovino around 1540.

Through lack of funds, the magnificent façade that was originally planned never came to pass and the interior decoration has also disappeared over time; the building, which has the second largest hall in the city (after the Maggior Consiglio in the Doge's Palace) is currently being converted into a cultural center. Facing the "New School" is the mighty, three-arched loggia of Palazzo Lezze, the work of Baldassare Longhena. Marking the beginning of the Fondamente Nuove, the Sacca della Misericordia is a square port area to the north of the district, originally used to store wood.

THE HIGHLIGHTS:
CANNAREGIO

TIP Paolo Olbi

Water, melancholy, a whiff of degeneracy – there are many such little corners, canals, and old *palazzi* in Venice (below). The church of Santa Maria dei Miracoli is a Renaissance treasure house (below right). Right, from left: The façade of the Jesuit church in the Fondamente Nuove is decorated with angels; magnificent frescoes grace its interior.

The Olbi family firm specializes in marbled paper and fine leather goods. Situated directly behind Santa Maria dei Miracoli, the extensive range can be enjoyed in slightly more relaxed surroundings than in the main store in San Marco.
Campo S. Maria Nova; Tel (041) 528 50 25; Mon–Fri 9.00–13.00

The baroque Jesuit church, known as Gesuiti, built at the start of the 18th century by Domenico Rossi, is dedicated to Santa Maria Assunta. The charming interior is clad in white and green marble, and bright frescoes by Louis Dorigny and Francesco Fontebasso decorate the vaults of the nave and choir. The high baroque altar is the work of Giuseppe Pozzo. Tintoretto's *Assumption of the Virgin* draws the gaze to the Lady Chapel altar in the left transept, but the church's artistic masterpiece is Titian's *Martyrdom of St Lawrence*. Construction of the church of Santa Maria dei Miracoli was overseen by Pietro Lombardo and his sons at the end of the 15th century. This single-naved church has a barrel vault and a raised square choir with a dome, but its most impressive feature is the elegant marble façade.

CASTELLO

The district of Castello, located to the east of San Marco, is the largest *sestiere* in Venice. Its name is derived from the fortifications established here as early as the 8th century. Before the advent of St Mark's, Castello was the spiritual hub of the Republic, and the church of San Pietro was the official cathedral of the diocese of Venice until 1807. The city's military strength in the Middle Ages and early modern period had its roots in this area, and the fleets of ships that made Venice the greatest sea power in the Mediterranean were made here, in the Arsenale. Now used as an Italian naval base, the Arsenale is closed to the public, but close by is the Naval History Museum, which houses a collection of model ships.

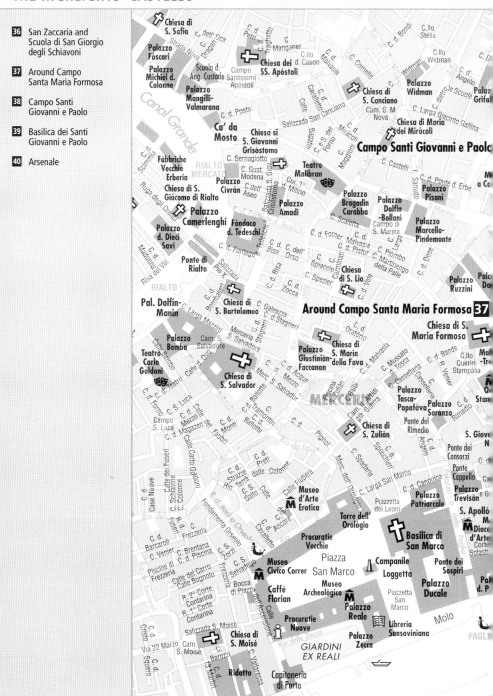

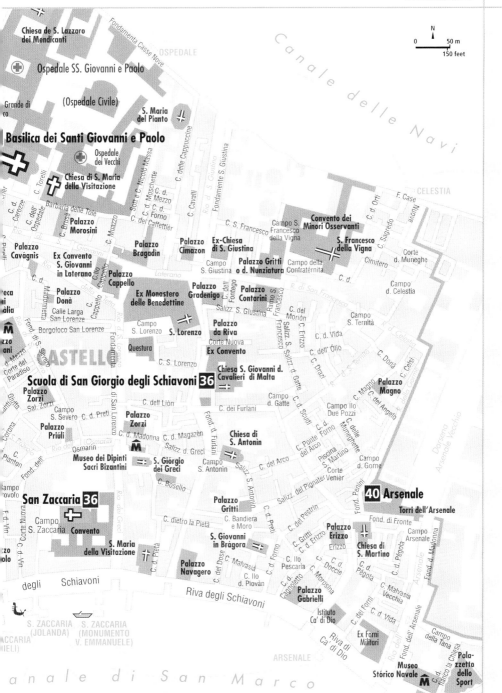

Chiesa de S. Lazzaro
dei Mendicanti

OSPEDALE

Ospedale SS. Giovanni e Paolo

Canale delle Navi

(Ospedale Civile)

Grande di
co

S. Maria
del Pianto

Basilica dei Santi Giovanni e Paolo

Ospedale
dei Vecchi

CELESTIA

Chiesa di S. Maria
della Visitazione

F. Case

Barbaria delle Tole

Convento dei
Minori Osservanti

Palazzo
Morosini

C. S. Francesco

Campo S.
Francesco
della Vigna

S. Francesco
della Vigna

Corte
d. Muneghe

Palazzo
Cavàgnis

Palazzo
Bragadin

Palazzo
Cimazon

Ex-Chiesa
di S. Giustina

Cimitero

Ex Convento
S. Giovanni
in Laterano

Campo
S. Giustina

Palazzo Gritti
o d. Nunziatura

Campo della
Contratérnita

Campo
d. Celestia

Palazzo
Cappello

Palazzo
Gradenigo

Palazzo
Contarini

Palazzo
Donà

Ex Monastero
delle Benedettine

eca
i
àlia

Salizz. S. Giustina

Campo
S. Ternità

Calle Larga
San Lorenzo

Campo
S. Lorenzo

Palazzo
da Riva

zzo
ani

Borgoloco San Lorenzo

S. Lorenzo

Corte Nuova

CASTELL

Questura

Ex Convento

C. S. Lorenzo

Chiesa S. Giovanni d.
Cavalieri di Malta

Palazzo
Magno

Scuola di San Giorgio degli Schiavoni 36

Palazzo
Zorzi

Campo
S. Severo

C. d. Preti

Campo
d. Gatte

Campo Ilo
Due Pozzi

C. dei Furlani

Palazzo
Zorzi

Palazzo
Priúli

Chiesa di
S. Antonin

Museo dei Dipinti
Sacri Bizantini

S. Giórgio
dei Greci

Campo
S. Antonin

Campo
d. Gorne

San Zaccaria 36

Palazzo
Gritti

40 Arsenale

Campo
S. Zaccaria

Convento

C. dietro la Pietà

C. Bandiera
e Moro

Palazzo
Erizzo

Torri dell'Arsenale

Campo
Arsenale

zo
olo

S. Maria
della Visitazione

S. Giovanni
in Brágora

Chiesa di
S. Martino

Palazzo
Navagero

degli

Schiavoni

Palazzo
Gabrielli

Riva degli Schiavoni

S. ZACCARIA
(JOLANDA)

S. ZACCARIA
(MONUMENTO
V. EMMANUELE)

Istituto
Ca' di Dio

ACCARIA
IELI)

Ex Forni
Militari

Campo
della Tana

ARSENALE

Museo
Stórico Navale

Pala-
zzetto
dello
Sport

anale di San Marco

THE HIGHLIGHTS: CASTELLO

The oldest part of the church of San Zaccaria (below right) is the 11th-century crypt, and its main attraction is Giovanni Bellini's painting, *Sacra Conversazione* (below). *The Triumph of St George* (right) is just part of Vittore Carpaccio's magnificent series of pictures in the small Scuola di San Giorgio degli Schiavoni.

INFO Icon collection

The Museo Dipinti Sacri Bizantini houses the Hellenic Institute's collection of icons, the largest in Europe, with 377 pieces, amply illustrating the Byzantine influence on Venetian art.
Campo dei Greci;
Tel (041) 522 65 81; Mon–Sat
9.00–17.00, last admission 16.00.

SAN ZACCARIA AND SCUOLA DI SAN GIORGIO DEGLI SCHIAVONI

The three-naved basilica of San Zaccaria has a polygonal choir and an ambulatory with apsidal chapels. It was given its current slant in the 15th century by Mauro Codussi, who succeeded in harmonizing his Renaissance-style upper levels with the high Gothic architecture of his dead predecessor, Antonio Gambello. The Scuola di San Giorgio degli Schiavoni was founded by a confraternity of merchants who emigrated from Dalmatia (Schiavonia). They decorated their headquarters lavishly: starting in 1501, Vittore Carpaccio created a series of ten paintings over the course of a decade, illustrating the lives of three saints with a lively and impressive realism, especially in the depictions of St George killing a dragon and St Hieronymus in his study. The interior is in a Renaissance style.

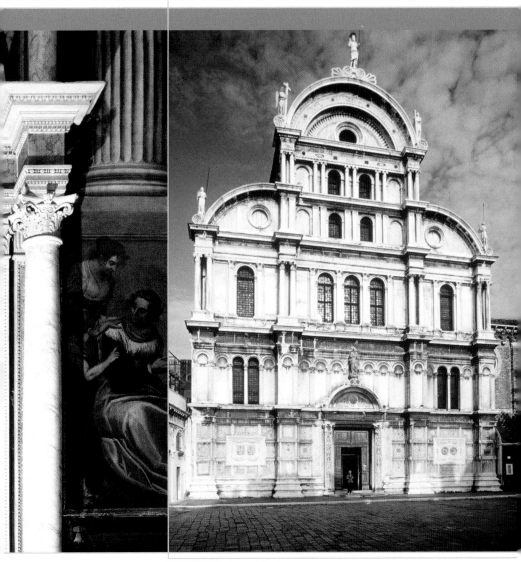

THE HIGHLIGHTS: CASTELLO

The Arco del Paradiso with its Virgin of Mercy and the Rio di Santa Maria Formosa (below middle and right). Insets below, from top: Campo Santa Maria Formosa and its eponymous church; Palazzo Querini-Stampalia, refurbished by Carlo Scarpia in 1968; within, Giovanni Bellini's picture, *The Presentation of Jesus at the Temple* (1460).

INFO Garden

The modern entrance hall (right) and Japanese-inspired garden, both designed by Carlo Scarpia, are a contrast to the 18th-century Palazzo Querini-Stampalia. Scarpa's pupil, Mario Botta, designed the cafeteria. *Santa Maria Formosa; Tel (041) 271 14 11; Tues–Sat 10.00–20.00, Sun 10.00–19.00.*

Campo Santa Maria Formosa is lined with magnificent *palazzi*. Palazzo Vitturi, originally laid out before the Gothic period, Sebastiano Venier's *palazzo*, and the Gothic lines of Palazzo Donà all lie to the east. To the north, the adjoining 17th-century Palazzo Priuli Ruzzini Loredan displays a mixture of mannerist elements. The 16th-century Renaissance Palazzo Malipiero stands to the south of the *campo* and the church of Santa Maria Formosa, built by Mauro Codussi at the end of the 15th century, is situated in the south-western corner of the square. Situated to the south of the square, the 16th-century Palazzo Querini-Stampalia boasts an interior decorated in the full pomp of the 18th century, in particular the wedding chamber (1790) with frescoes by Jacopo Guarana. The Querini family art collection of Venetian Old Masters is quite captivating.

THE HIGHLIGHTS: CASTELLO

With its late Gothic portal created by Bartolomeo Bon, the mighty edifice of the church of Santi Giovanni e Paolo commands the square (below), in the middle of which stands the imposing equestrian statue of Condottiere Bartolomeo Colleoni. The statue was completed according to a design by Verrocchio in 1496 (below right).

TIP Rosa Salva

The Rosa family has been serving customers since 1870, and today Rosa Salva is famed for her excellent patisserie. This branch is also known to fans of crime fiction as Commissario Brunetti's preferred café.
Campo Santi Giovanni e Paolo; Tel (041) 522 79 49; Mon–Sat 8.00–20.00.

This square, one of the most striking in Venice, is marked by three monuments: the brick Gothic Dominican church of Santi Giovanni e Paolo, the *Scuola* Grande di San Marco, and Andrea del Verrocchio's enormous equestrian statue of the mercenary warrior, Bartolomeo Colleoni. The scuola, built by Pietro Lombardo and Mauro Codussi, is considered a masterpiece of early Renaissance Venetian architecture. Originally owned by the Confraternity of St Mark, the building has been used for charitable purposes since its completion in the 15th century – it is presently run as a clinic. Most of the art treasures that once graced its walls have disappeared, apart from two paintings by Veronese and Tintoretto. Fortunately, the wooden ceiling in the impressive 16th-century library has survived. The Church of Santi Giovanni e Paolo contains the tombs of twenty-five of Venice's doges up to the year 1700.

THE HIGHLIGHTS: CASTELLO

TIP Osteria al Ponte

According to an inscription, the nave of the Dominican church with its columns was completed in 1369 (below). The interior reveals numerous wall burial vaults (right), including the tomb of Doge Tomaso Mocenigo, topped with a baldachin, which was completed just as the Gothic period gave way to the Renaissance (below right).

A stone's throw from San Zanipolo, by the Ponte del Cavallo, this is a small *osteria* where you can easily feel at home, surrounded by dyed-in-the-wool Venetians. A wide selection of snacks and good wines is available at reasonable prices. *Ponte del Cavallo; Tel (041) 528 61 57); 8.00–21.00, daily.*

Known locally as San Zanipolo, this three-aisled, Gothic pillar basilica with a quatrefoil cupola is Venice's largest religious building. The ribbed vaulting in the nave is some 35 m (115 feet) high. San Zanipolo was the sepulchre of choice for Venetian rulers: the tombs of 25 doges can be found here, of which the Gothic wall tombs of Michele Morosini and Tomaso Mocenigo are the most exceptional. The Renaissance tombs of Nicolò Marcello and Pietro Mocenigo, constructed by Pietro Lombardo, and that of Andrea Vendramin, built by Tullio Lombar, are also well worth seeing. Other sights include Baldassare Longhena's baroque high altar, a polyptych created by Giovanni Bellini, and Giovanni Battista Piazzetta's ceiling located in the Cappella di San Domenico. The painting *The Adoration of the Shepherds* in the Cappella del Rosario is one of Veronese's masterpieces.

THE HIGHLIGHTS: CASTELLO

INFO Museo Storico Navale

The pedestrian entrance to the Arsenale is guarded by St Mark's winged lion, which also stands beside the twin towers of the canal entrance (below). During the Biennale, modern art is exhibited in the ancient halls of the Arsenale (below right). Right: A 17th-century plan of the Arsenale, now kept in the Museo Storico Navale.

The naval history of the Venetian Republic, with model ships, war booty, weapons, and the doge's ceremonial barge (inset, below left). Modern exhibits include manned torpedoes from World War II.
Riva San Biagio; Tel (041) 520 02 76; Mon–Fri 8.45–13.30, Sat 8.45–13.00, closed Sun.

At more than 32 ha (80 acres) in size, the Arsenale covers most of the suburb of Castello. Laid out as a shipyard, weapons store, and naval strongpoint in 1104, this area was at the heart of Venetian shipbuilding, expanding as the naval fleet collected victories and the merchant fleet grew in importance. Eulogized by Dante in his *Divine Comedy*, the Arsenale employed up to 30,000 workers and was renowned for the solidity of its shipbuilding, securing the Venetians great advantages in the Crusades and the wars against the Turks. The division of labor utilized in its approach to manufacturing was to become the basis for modern production-line techniques. Of the fortifications that once surrounded the shipyard, there remain only the 15th-century land entrance, the Ingresso di Terra, and the 16th-century quayside gate, the Ingresso all'Acqua. Much was destroyed during Napoleon's time.

Faces, faces: this installation by Nancy Spero (below) was the topic of much discussion at the 2007 Biennale. Insets below right, from top: The entrances to the British, Nordic (Finland, Norway, Sweden), and German pavilions. Right, from left: Hollywood royalty at the Film Festival in 2008: Tilda Swinton, Brad Pitt, and George Clooney; Anne Hathaway on the red carpet.

ART SCENE RENDEZVOUS: BIENNALE DI VENEZIA

The Biennale di Venezia, Venice's international art exhibition, has been held between June and October in every odd year since 1895, with a six-year break during World War II. Since the beginning of the 20th century, national pavilions have been erected in the Giardini Pubblici, parks laid out in 1807 around the Palazzo dell'Esposizione in Castello, and the leading artists of each country have exhibited their work. Since then, the 16th-century halls of the Arsenale have also been used as exhibition space. Other exhibition venues for the participating nations are distributed right across the city. The Architecture Biennale has been held in the even years for the last few decades, and the International Film Festival, instituted in 1932 under the aegis of the Biennale, is held annually on the Lido, in August and September. Biennale events have always attracted media attention, such as in 1970, when the artist Günther Uecker drove a nail into a pillar in the portico of the German pavilion to highlight the martial aesthetic of the building, which had been refurbished in 1938 during the Nazi period. The Biennale and the Film Festival are important sources of revenue for the city, attracting thousands of visitors wishing both to enjoy contemporary art and to attend a great festival.

THE HIGHLIGHTS

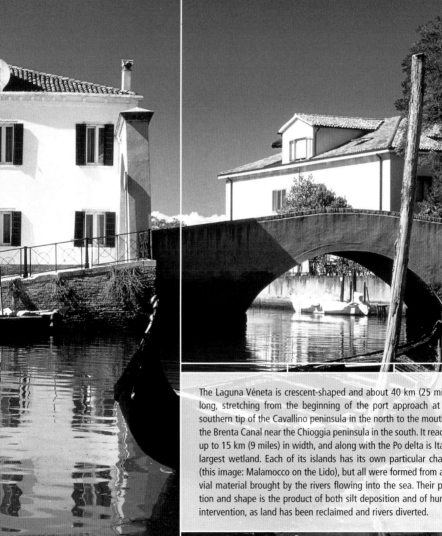

THE LAGOON ISLANDS AND THE BRENTA CANAL

The Laguna Véneta is crescent-shaped and about 40 km (25 miles) long, stretching from the beginning of the port approach at the southern tip of the Cavallino peninsula in the north to the mouth of the Brenta Canal near the Chioggia peninsula in the south. It reaches up to 15 km (9 miles) in width, and along with the Po delta is Italy's largest wetland. Each of its islands has its own particular charms (this image: Malamocco on the Lido), but all were formed from alluvial material brought by the rivers flowing into the sea. Their position and shape is the product of both silt deposition and of human intervention, as land has been reclaimed and rivers diverted.

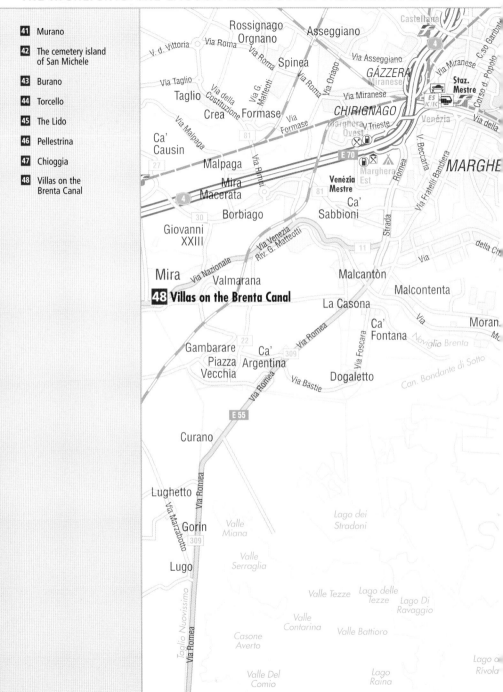

LA CERVA

Tessera

Aeroporto Marco Polo

Palude del Monte

Torcello 44

V. Martiri d.

Via

Libertà

Via Orlanda

Osellino

Punta Lunga

Í. Buèl del Lovo

Mazzorbo

Mazzorbo

Burano

ola

ESTRE

Gobbi

Can.

Via Libertà

Via Orlanda

CAMPALTO

Burano 43

Í. di Crevan

P.to ghéra

Porto di Campalto

Laguna Véneta

Can. di S.Maria

Sant' Erasmo

VERNIER

Museo del Vetro

SANT'ERASMO

Murano 41

LE VIGNOLE

Punta Sabbioni

Porto Marghera

Í. del Tronchetto

Staz. S. Lucia

Can. delle Sacche

Staz. Marittima

42 Cemetery island of San Michele

LA CERTOSA

Ponte della Libertà

Ponte di Rialto

ES IC/EC

VENÉZIA

Ca' Rezzonico

Basilica di S. Marco

Aeroporto G. Nicelli

Fond. Zattere P. Lungo

Palazzo Ducale

Biennale

Stadio Sant'Elena

S. NICOLÒ

Can. della Giudecca

S. Nicolò

LA GIUDECCA

Sacca Fisola

Í. la Grazia

Í. S. Servolo

The Lido 45

Riv.

Golfo

na

Í. S. Clemente

Casinò Municipale

G. Marconi

Sacca Sessola

Palazzo del Cinema, Teatro Perla

Lungomare

di

Í. S. Spirito

Via Sandro Gallo

Littorale di Lido

e di Volpego

Laguna Véneta

Ísola Poveglia

Golfo

MALAMOCCO

Via Malamocco

di

Venézia

ALBERONI

N

0   2 km

Pellestrina 46 ↓   ↓ **47 Chioggia**

1 mile

INFO Museo del Vetro

The Basilica dei Santi Maria e Donato on Murano has an impressive two-floor choir area (below) and a 12th-century mosaic floor (inset, below left). The biggest attractions on the cemetery island of San Michele are the church of San Michele in Isola and the Cappella Emiliana (below right).

The Glass Museum is housed in Palazzo Giustinian, a stone's throw from the *vaporetto* stop. The exhibition illustrates 2,000 years of glassblowing and there are several masterpieces of Venetian glassware in the collection.
Fondamenta Giustinian; Tel (041) 73 95 86; Thurs–Tues 10.00–16.00.

Visiting Murano is worthwhile, and not just for the objects made from locally produced glass that are made here. The 12th-century Basilica dei Santi Maria e Donato with its colonnaded choir and brilliant mosaics is also worth seeing, as is the Gothic Palazzo di Mula, one of the last remaining summer residences once used by wealthy Venetians. The cemetery island of San Michele was once the site of a Camaldolite monastery. In 1469 Mauro Codussi began construction work on the Renaissance church of San Michele in Isola and Guglielmo Bergam-asco built the Cappella Emiliana only a little later. The monastery was dissolved in the time of Napoleon, being replaced by a walled cemetery. Celebrities such as Ezra Pound, Joseph Brodsky, and Igor Stravinsky have all found a last resting place here.

Hot work on Murano: glass is produced by melting silica, sodium carbonate, lime, and various metal oxides (which determine the coloration) to 1,370 °C. Only then can the *maestro vetraio* begin the art of glassblowing. Shears and tongs are used to shape the piece. Below: Valuable goblets and a detail of a sculpture of Poseidon and a nymph.

MURANO GLASS

The art of glassblowing experienced its heyday during the Roman period, but the techniques for producing thin-walled, stained glass were lost in the confusion caused during the later "great migrations". The Middle Ages and the advent of artisans from Constantinople were to reacquaint the Venetians with skilled glass production, however, and Venice soon became "Europe's City of Glass". The furnaces, initially operated by glassblowers in the north of the city, were often the cause of fires. For this reason, and to preserve the secret of stained glass production, betrayal of which was punishable by death, the trade was moved to the island of Murano in the 13th century. The industry is still the principal source of revenue for the island, and tourists are greeted with objects of the finest quality, from paperweights and glasses and vases to modern *objets d'art*. Murano has specialized in the manufacture of chandeliers for centuries and these hang in many of the *palazzi* of Venice; the entrance hall of the Museo del Vetro in Palazzo Giustinian on Murano has three such magnificent chandeliers for visitors to admire. One was produced in 1854 in the workshop of the Fratelli Toso, who are still the leading firm of glass manufacturers on the lagoon.

THE HIGHLIGHTS:
THE LAGOON ISLANDS
AND THE BRENTA CANAL

Burano still shows traces of the idyllic old fishing community it once was, and these brightly painted fishermen's cottages (below right) are typical of this picturesque island. The slightly crooked campanile of the church of San Martino (below) can be seen from afar.

INFO Museo del Merletto

The old lacemaking school houses a museum exhibiting more than 100 hand-made pieces of Venetian lace from four centuries. The lacemakers can be seen at work in the mornings.
Piazza Galuppi 187; Tel (041) 73 00 34; Wed–Mon 1 Apr–2 Nov 10.00–17.00, 3 Nov–31 Mar 10.00–16.00.

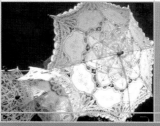

The island of Burano, with its long rows of brightly painted houses that line the canals, is one of the most picturesque spots in the whole lagoon. The island is located south of Torcello and is connected to the island of Mazzorbo by a wooden bridge. For a long time it was the men and their fishing boats that supported the islanders, but nowadays it is the women who are famed for their lacemaking. They developed a laborious technique known as *reticella*, which characteristically uses double stitching, *punto in aria* ("air stitches") in geometric patterns, often of Oriental origin. Burano became a byword for fine lace crafted with yellow silk, and this traditional and skilled handicraft was able to compete even in the age of industrial lace production, aided in no small way by the foundation of a lacemaking school, the Scuola dei Merletti, in 1872, which is housed in the Palazzo del Podestà.

The baptistry of Santa Fosca and the cathedral of Santa Maria Assunta date back to Torcello's time as a diocese (right). Amongst the cathedral's treasures are the rood screen with panels depicting St Mary and the saints (below), and the *Last Judgment* on the west wall (below right).

INFO Museo dell'Estuario

In 1870 Count Torelli donated a collection of archeological finds from the lagoon. The treasures include Etruscan and Roman pottery, early bronze finds, mosaics, and gold ornaments.
Palazzo del Consiglio;
Tel (041) 73 07 61; Tues–Sun
10.30–12.30, 14.00–16.00

Torcello lies in the north of the lagoon and was one of the first islands to be settled. In the 7th century it became the seat of the bishop of Altinum, experiencing its heyday in the early Middle Ages but eventually falling victim to the lagoon's silt. The religious buildings here bear witness to Torcello's former greatness: the cathedral of Santa Maria Assunta was consecrated in 1008, and both the cathedral and the adjoining church of Santa Fosca are masterpieces of Byzantine architecture. The apse of the cathedral is adorned with one of the most beautiful examples of mosaic work in Venice, a Madonna created at some point during the 12th or 13th centuries, and opposite this there is a huge mosaic of the Last Judgement. Masonry from an older church has been incorporated into the marble chancel and a simple stone bench in front of the building is said to have been used as a throne by Attila, King of the Huns.

THE HIGHLIGHTS:
THE LAGOON ISLANDS
AND THE BRENTA CANAL

INFO Jewish Cemetery

Legendary palatial hotels like the Excelsior (below) recall a time when all of Europe's high society congregated here. Thomas Mann stayed at the Grand Hotel des Bains, as did Luchino Visconti, although much later. The International Film Festival's Golden Lion (right) is awarded every fall in the Palazzo del Cinema.

Great literary figures such as Goethe, Shelley, and Keats loved the peace of the Jewish cemetery. The oldest graves date from the 15th century. There are guided tours in English on Fridays at 10.30 and Sundays at 14.30.
Strada di San Nicolò;
Tel (041) 71 53 59.

Thomas Mann's *Death in Venice* (1912) immortalized the Lido as a place of luxurious decadence. Although the Grand Hotel Excelsior and the Hotel des Bains, in which Mann's novella is set, are still to be found, as are the blue-and-white-striped bathing huts from which the protagonist Aschen-bach observes the boy, Tadzio, the Lido has lost much of its urbane charm. The world's first bathing beach was opened on its 12 km (7.5 miles) of sandbanks in the 19th century, and by 1900 the Lido was one of the most fashionable bathing resorts in Europe. Nowadays, the Adriatic side is an over-crowded resort for tourists and Venetians alike. Only once a year does the Lido have a chance to recall its former elegance, when it becomes a catwalk for the celebrities attending the International Film Festival in August and September. The Lido also boasts the only golf course in Venice.

TIP The fish market

On Pellestrina, fantastic fish is to be found in San Pietro in Volta, and the plot of Donna Leon's detective novel, *A Sea Of Troubles*, is mostly set amongst the fishermen here (below right, from top). The Chioggia peninsula is the scene of a comedy by the playwright, Carlo Goldoni. Below: Chioggia port.

Italy's largest fish market is a real attraction and an appetizing sight. On every day except Sunday, fishermen sell fresh seafood of all kinds on the Corso del Popolo from 6.00 until 13.30. Inveterate early risers can go and experience the auctions here – as long as they keep quiet!

Pellestrina is almost as long as the Lido, but in places is less than 100 m (328 feet) across. That this island has not long since fallen back into the sea is due to the high *murazzi*, 18th-century marble walls erected on the Adriatic side. The mainland begins a little to the south of the island. The Chioggia peninsula has belonged to La Serenissima since the war with Genoa in 1380. Chioggia's long history as a diocese is witnessed by the 12th-century cathedral of Santa Maria Assunta, which was refurbished in the 17th century by Baldassare Longhena and now houses works by Palma Giovane, Domenico Negri, and Cima da Conegliano. The downtown of Chioggia around the Corso del Popolo has picturesque buildings and many bars, and is popular with tourists, as is the sandy beach of Sottomarina.

THE HIGHLIGHTS: THE LAGOON ISLANDS AND THE BRENTA CANAL

Over 150 villas bear witness to the former wealth of the Venetians on the Riviera del Brenta, the banks of the Brenta Canal. Work on the Villa Contarini-Camerini was begun in 1546 and continued into the 17th century (below). The Villa Foscari was designed by the great architect, Andrea Palladio (below right).

INFO Trips on the Brenta

The stylishly fitted-out motorboat Il Burchiello plies the Brenta between Venice and Padua. There are 50 villas on the stretch of the canal and three of the most famous summer residences can be visited as part of the cruise.
Tel (049) 820 69 10; Mar–Oct.
www.ilburchiello.it

Some 33 km (20 miles) of the Brenta River were canalized in the 16th century to make a navigable connection between Venice and Padua, and wealthy Venetians had enormous country houses built on the banks of the canal. Travel up the canal from the lagoon and just by the hamlet of Fusina you'll find the Villa Foscari, also known as La Malcontenta, which was built around 1560 to a design by Andrea Palladio with frescoes by Giovanni Battista Zelotti. The little town of Mira also boasts several *palazzi*, of which the most picturesque is the Villa Widmann Foscari, built in a rococo style by Alessandro Tirali with frescoes by Giuseppe Angeli and Gerolamo Mengozzi. The most imposing building on the Riviera del Brenta is the overhanging Villa Pisani, just before Padua. Its ballroom has ceiling frescoes by Giovanni Battista Tiepolo, and in 1934 it was the scene of Hitler and Mussolini's first meeting.

COMPACT
VENICE

Part of Venice's charm is that there are no cars. As humorist Robert Benchley famously cabled on arrival, "Streets filled with water. Please advise." It is one of the most fascinating cities in the world and its fairytale atmosphere has been captivating visitors for centuries. Palaces, churches, museums, walks, and boat trips are some of the highlights. Magnificent theaters, galleries of international renown, smart stores, bars and cafés, *trattorie*, and fine restaurants offer the visitor an almost 24-hour itinerary. There is a range of accommodation, from small pensions to luxury hotels, and as well as the revived Carnival there is always a regatta or an event on.

Museums, music, and drama

Museo Fortuny
Hailing from Spain, Mariano Fortuny (1871–1949) was a *fin de siècle* polymath and artist with many interests and skills. He enjoyed painting, sculpting, photography, and design of various items, such as stage sets, lamps, beautifully patterned cloths, and imaginative silk dresses. His late Gothic *palazzo* was donated to the city by his widow and exhibits works in memory of this versatile artist and his workshop.
San Marco 3958, 30124 Venezia; Tel 041/520 09 95; Wed–Mon 10.00–18.00, closed 1 Jan, 1 May, 25 Dec. www.museicivicivenezian.it

Teatro Carlo Goldoni
The Teatro Vendramin near the Rialto Bridge was founded in 1622, changing its name to the Teatro Carlo Goldoni in 1875. The attractive auditorium has boxes and about 800 seats, and plays, ballets, and concerts are performed.

St Mark's Basilica: gilt mosaic *The Last Judgment* (1816).

San Marco 4650 b, Calle Goldoni; Tel 041/520 54 22. www.italianticketoffice.it

Festivals and events

Venice Carnival
Venice has been celebrating Carnival for 900 years. This period of high jinks that has turned into an international event begins on the Sunday before "mad Thursday" and is marked by the descent of an acrobat – in days gone by it was a dove made of papier mâché – from the Campanile to the Doge's Palace. Although many Venetians themselves take a back seat, around 150,000 people from all over the world find their way into the city's squares and streets. Carnival disappeared from the calendar with the demise of the Republic in 1797 and was revived only in 1979, attracting ever more tourists every year since then. Many enthusiasts disguise themselves with elaborate costumes and masks based on the Commedia dell'Arte, attracting the lenses of countless photographers (see p. 32).
Feb/Mar.
www.carnivalofvenice.com

Su e Zo per i Ponti
This run "back and forth across the bridges" has been taking place for over 20 years. The run starts at the Doge's Palace.
2nd Sun in Mar.

Benedizione del Fuoco
Visitors to Venice during Holy Week should certainly try to experience the Blessing of Fire in St Mark's Basilica. The interior of the Basilica is darkened on the afternoon of Maundy Thursday. During the ceremony, the holy flame is lit in the atrium and carried through the building as the candles throughout the church are gradually all lit as well, until the whole Basilica is flooded with warm, soft candlelight.
Easter: late afternoon on Maundy Thursday.

Festa di San Marco
St Mark's Day, which is coincidentally also Liberation Day, an Italian public holiday, is celebrated to commemorate the day on which the relics of the city's patron saint were brought from Alexandria in Egypt to Venice in 828. A solemn mass is held in the Basilica, but St Mark's Square is always full of merrymakers.
25 Apr.

Sport and leisure

Disney Store
Everything likely to excite Disney fans large and small – Mickey Mouse greets visitors of all sizes on a Venetian bridge, whilst Donald Duck sits in a boat on the canal and fishes.
Campo San Bartolomeo; Tel 041/522 39 80.

Shopping

Antiques fair
An antiques fair is held three times a year in Campo San Maurizio. Numerous dealers come from far and wide, and Venice rarely if ever has so many very fine pieces for sale. There are beads, glassware, all sorts of paintings (especially views of Venice), and any number of old utensils, as well as lots of kitsch. Don't expect to pick up many bargains, though.
Campo San Maurizio; Tel 041/98 88 10; Fri–Sun, three times a year (the weekend before Easter, the 4th weekend in Sept and the weekend before Christmas).

Arcobaleno Pigmenti
Run by Massimo Nube, this store seems at first glance to be small and unassuming. A second glance reveals it to be heaven for artists, especially painters: powdered paint of almost every shade is stored in countless containers, as well as glues and all sorts of artist's requisites. Not exactly cheap.
Calle delle Botteghe, San Marco 3457; Tel 041/523 68 18.

Legatoria Piazzasi
One of the oldest sites for the manufacture of a traditional Venetian product: beautiful and unusual paper, in the form of bookmarks, notebooks, diaries, and much more. There's a present from

From left: A baroque con-glomeration: an antiques shop in San Marco; the loggetta of St Mark's cam-panile; the magnificence of the Museo Fortuny; the ele-gantly decorated Heming-way Suite in the Gritti Palace.

These pages give additional information for the area described in the "Highlights" chapter (pp. 20–55).

Venice to be found here for everyone.
Campiello della Feltrina, San Marco 2511 c;
Tel 041/522 12 02;
Mon–Sat 11.00–13.00, 15.00–19.00.
www.legatoriapiazzasi.it

Perle e Dintorni
As the glass industry is based in nearby Murano, there are plenty of bead shops in the town; you can assemble glass beads to your own taste in this store. Make a gift for yourself or others from the wide range of dazzling beads on offer.
Calle della Mandola, San Marco 3740;
Tel 041/71 00 31.
www.perle-e-dintorni.it

Rolando Segalin
This shoe *atelier* produces smart, handmade fitted shoes, although only to order. The store also stocks beautiful factory-made shoes. Not very cheap, but Italian shoemaking skill is always a temptation.
Calle dei Fuseri, San Marco 4365;
Tel 041/522 21 15;
Mon–Fri 9.00–12.30, 16.00–19.30, Sat 9.00–13.00.

Vivaldi
Cristiano Nalessi's store stocks everything you need as far as Vivaldi, the city's greatest baroque composer and conductor, is concerned. Apart from CDs of his music, there are also bags, pens, paper, and all sorts of useful and useless things with his picture on the front.
Salizada del Fontego dei Tedeschi, San Marco 5537;
Tel 041/252 13 43;
Mon–Sat 9.30–19.30, Sun 11.00–19.00.

Eating and drinking

Gelateria Paolin
Indulge yourself in the finest ice cream from one of the oldest ice-cream parlours in Venice.
Campo Santo Stefano, San Marco 2962.

Enoteca al Volto
A romantically atmospheric vault where you can choose from more than 1,000 wines, mostly of Italian provenance, whilst munching on a few little snacks.
Calle Cavalli, San Marco 30124;
Tel 041/522 89 45;
closed Sun and after 22.30.

Harry's Bar
The bar and its adjoining restaurant have become one of Venice's top tourist attrac-tions. Ernest Hemingway and many other famous people have sipped their drinks here or tried out the Bellini, the invention of Cipriani's bar-man and owner. Treat yourself to one of these not overly pricey cocktails made from prosecco and peach juice at the bar. Another of Cipriani's inventions has reached all corners of the world: *carpac-cio*, wafer-thin slices of raw beef scattered with freshly flaked Parmesan cheese, lent even greater refinement with a little olive oil.
Calle Vallaresso, San Marco 1323;
Tel 041/528 57 77.

Accommodation

Cavalletto & Doge Orseolo
Situated directly behind the Procuratie Vecchie; a good address and only a stone's throw from St Mark's Square.

This Best Western Hotel occu-pies a building that was built in 1308 and refurbished in 2003. During breakfast you can watch the *gondolieri* preparing their boats for the onslaught of tourists.
Calle Cavalletto, San Marco 1107;
Tel 041/520 09 55.
www.cavalletto.hotelinvenic e.com

Concordia
It must be impossible to spend a night closer to St Mark's than this. A comfort-able hotel with good service, where you can enjoy the scenery of St Mark's Square even during breakfast. No other hotel in Venice has a view like this. Run by the Beg-giato family for four genera-tions, the hotel is decorated with period furniture and Murano chandeliers.
Calle Larga, San Marco 367;
Tel 041/520 68 66.
www.hotelconcordia.it

Gritti Palace
A Renaissance palace built in the early 16th century for the doge, Andrea Gritti, and pre-sented to the pope, Sixtus V, in 1585. Many famous people have spent the night here, including the literary giants Hemingway and Simenon. The service in this traditional establishment, located near the Grand Canal and one of the finest hotels in the world, is excellent. Reasonably inti-mate in size (91 rooms), it is one of the best hotels in the city. All the rooms are differ-ent, but the best ones over-look the Grand Canal. Eating on the terrace overlooking the canal when the weather is warm is an experience not to be missed.

Campo Santa Maria del Giglio, San Marco 2467;
Tel 041/79 46 11. www. gritti.hotelinvenice.com

Serenissima
Situated centrally between the Rialto Bridge and St Mark's Square, this hotel offers good value for money and has been run by the del Borgo family for many years. The walls are decorated with modern art and there is a bar in the foyer should you care for an evening drink. The windows of some of the rooms open onto a little inner courtyard.
Calle Goldoni, San Marco 4486;
Tel 041/520 00 11.
www.hotelserenissima.it

Nightlife

Teatro San Gallo
A lavish meal of typical Vene-tian delicacies, followed by a captivating show with music, drama, and a spectacular light show. Illustrating the history of Carnival in Venice, the performance is called "Carnival – The Show" and is translated into various lan-guages. The afternoon shows are about a third cheaper than the slightly longer evening performances. Live performers combine with screen projections to bring the city's past to life along with famous personalities associated with Venice such as Marco Polo, Casanova, and Lord Byron.
Campo San Gallo o Canova, San Marco 1098;
Tel 041/241 19 43;
Sun–Thurs 19.30,
Fri, Sat two performances at 18.45 and 21.00. www. venice-carnival-show.com

Museums, music and drama

Museo di Storia Naturale
The Natural History Museum in the Fondaco dei Turchi has a wide collection of scientific and natural history exhibits, from dinosaurs to the flora and fauna of the lagoon.
Santa Croce 1730;
Tel 041/275 02 06;
Tues–Fri 9.00–13.00,
Sat, Sun 10.00–16.00,
closed 1 Jan,
1 May, 25 Dec.
www.museiciviciveneziani.it

Galleria Internazionale d'Arte Moderna Ca' Pesaro
The museum of modern art came into being as a result of municipal purchases made during the Biennale and donations from collectors. It houses famous works by international artists such as Rodin, Klimt, Kandinsky, Chagall, and Miró, as well as

Thinking man's art: Rodin's
***The Thinker* in the Ca' Pesaro.**

works by Italian masters such as De Chirico, Carrà, and Morandi (see p. 68).
Ca' Pesaro, Santa Croce 2076;
Tel 041/72 11 27;
Apr–Oct Tues–Sun
10.00–18.00,
Nov–Mar 10.00–17.00,
closed 1 Jan, 1 May, 25 Dec.
www.museiciviciveneziani.it

Museo d'Arte Orientale
This state museum is also housed in the Ca' Pesaro and possesses an important collection of Japanese and Chinese art, as well as many exquisite handicraft objects.
Ca' Pesaro, Santa Croce 2076; Tel 041/520 03 45;
Tues–Sun 10.00–17.00,
closed 1 Jan, 1 May, 25 Dec.
www.artive.arti.benecultur ali.it

Galleria Giorgio Franchetti, Ca' d'Oro
Baron Giorgio Franchetti donated this splendid palace and its magnificent art collection to the state in 1915. Such Italian masters as Giovanni Bellini, Vittore Carpaccio, Mantegna, Giorgione, Titian, Tintoretto, and Francesco Guardi can be admired here, as well as Flemish painting, Gobelin tapestry, and great sculptures.
Cannaregio 3932;
Tel. 041/522 23 49;
Mon 8.15–14.00,
Tues–Thurs 8.15–19.15,
closed 1 Jan, 25 Dec.
www.cadoro.org

Festivals and events

Regata della Befana
Befane is a good witch, surprising well-behaved children with presents of all sizes and shapes, which she brings into the house down the chimney.

There is a rowing regatta on the Grand Canal dedicated to her, where the teams dress up as witches. This is the early beginning of the long Venetian regatta season, which includes a variety of events.
6 Jan.

Regata storica
An extensive and striking spectacle that takes place on the Grand Canal. First there is a procession of historic ships, which is best enjoyed from a boat on the canal, as the few seats on the banks are usually taken. The teams in the boats then dress up in historical costumes as the various city districts and islands compete in various rowing events in a generally relaxed party atmosphere.
1st Sun in Sept.

Festa della Madonna
As with the Festa del Redentore, this feast day can be traced back to a plague epidemic in 1630. The procession leaves Santa Maria del Giglio and crosses a pontoon bridge over the Grand Canal to the square in front of the Salute church, where candles are lit. This is the signal to begin the feast proper, and *castradina* is served up; this is a dish of cooked smoked mutton with good helpings of Savoy cabbage and takes a bit of getting used to, but it is very authentic.
21 Nov.

Shopping

Aliani
A delicatessen by the book. A tremendously good selection of hams, sausages, smoked meats, and cheese that is so tempting that you

start to feel hungry as soon as you enter the shop.
Ruga Vecchia San Giovanni, San Polo 654;
Tel 041/522 49 13;
closed Sun.

Mauro el Forner de Canton
A fantastic bakery with the very best produce, both sweet and savory.
Strada Nova,
Cannaregio 3845;
Tel 041/522 29 68;
closed Sun.

Eating and drinking

Alla Botte
A meeting-place for tourists and locals alike, where you can drink an aperitif or a glass of wine at the long bar. The *osteria* has a good selection of various wines, to go with excellent *cicchetti* and local cuisine.
Calle della Bissa,
San Marco 5482;
Tel 041/520 97 75

All'Arco
A lot of greengrocers and fishmongers come in here for a little something or a coffee after the Rialto market. The little snacks, especially the *tramezzini* and the freshly made *panini*, are delicious.
Calle dell'Arco, San Polo 436; Tel 041/520 56 66;
Mon–Sat 7.00–17.00.

Osteria Antico Dolo
This has been many Venetians' regular bar since 1434. Have a glass of wine and enjoy the lovingly prepared *cicchetti* and the extremely appetizing nibbles: croquettes with tuna or octopus, stuffed olives, or *sarde in saor* (sardines pickled with onions, sultanas, and pine nuts).

From left: You might say that the Grand Canal is Venice's main road, and not just for the *gondolieri*; the Ca' Rezzonico seen from a *vaporetto*; a *traghetto* (gondola ferry) in action; the façade of the Bauer luxury hotel.

These pages give additional information for the area described in the "Highlights" chapter (pp. 56–73).

Ruga Vecchia San Giovanni,
San Polo 778;
Tel. 041/522 65 46;
Mon–Sat 12.00–15.00,
18.00–22.00.
www.anticodolo.it

Accommodation

Antica Locanda Sturion
This three-star hotel is located in a Renaissance *palazzo* with a view of the Grand Canal, and is right in the heart of the Rialto. Merchants, seafarers, ambassadors, and artists have all stayed here. The library has books about the history and art of Venice in various languages. The Bistrot de Venise in the Calle dei Fabbri is also part of the hotel and about ten minutes' walk away, and hotel residents have the benefit of a discount here.
Calle del Sturion,
San Polo 679; Hotel:
Tel 041/523 62 43,
Restaurant:
Tel 041/523 66 51.
www.locandasturion.com

Bauer Venezia
The Bauer luxury hotel of 91 rooms and 18 suites has a captivating location right beside the Grand Canal. The hotel, part of the "Leading Small Hotels of the World" group, has a gym and spa area, and the De Pisis restaurant boasts excellent cooking.
Campo San Moisè,
San Marco 1459;
Tel 041/520 70 22.
www.bauervenezia.com

Rialto
This four-star hotel with a view of the Rialto Bridge is in the very heart of the city. Whether minded for culture or headed for the market or shopping streets, you'll find everything reachable within minutes. Breakfast is served on a terrace with a panoramic view.
Ponte Rialto,
San Marco 5149;
Tel 041/520 91 66.
www.rialtohotel.com

Nightlife

I Musici Veneziani
The Scuola Grande di San Teodoro, a building once belonging to one of the great guilds, is the venue for excellent concerts, including works by Vivaldi, Albinoni, and Donizetti, as well as Mozart. The standard is very high and an excellent evening's music is guaranteed – and all at a good price!
Campo San Salvador;
Tel 041/521 02 94.

I Virtuosi di Venezia
There are amazing things to be heard from the San Marco chamber orchestra in the church of Ateneo di San Basso. The emphasis lies on the works of Antonio Vivaldi (including The Four Seasons, of course) and other baroque composers.
Ateneo di San Basso;
admission: 20.00,
concert begins: 20.30.
www.hellovenezia.i

Getting around

Traghetti
Manned by two oarsmen, the boats are normally old gondolas, stripped of their original rich decoration. Most *traghetti* have been operated by the same families for generations. In the 1950s, there were around 30 routes, but today there are just seven. Venice has to be experienced from the water. Three bridges span the Grand Canal and gondola ferries will take pedestrians across at a number of places, indicated by the *traghetto* sign; occasionally other gondolas are used. You pay on the ferry and usually travel standing up.
Open during business hours, closed Sun.

Water taxis
Motoscafi are small boats that can navigate even the smaller canals. They work just like taxis, i.e. with regulated fares and the taximeter is switched on at the beginning of the journey. A trip is expensive and really only worth it for groups, who also pay an extra charge if there are more than four people. There are also other extra charges, e.g. for luggage. The most important stands are at Marco Polo Airport, Piazzale Roma (car park), Rialto Bridge, and of course St Mark's.
Marco Polo Airport:
Tel 041/541 50 84;
railway station:
Tel 041/71 62 86;
Piazzale Roma:
Tel 041/716 922;
San Marco:
Tel 041/522 97 50.

Gondolas
The gondola is the traditional Venetian, flat-bottomed boat, painted black, as decreed by law. During the 18th century there were several thousand of them, but today just a few hundred remain. Originally the main means of transport for Venetians, they are now mostly hired by tourists, though a few are privately owned. Gondoliers have to follow an apprenticeship, after which they must pass an exam testing their knowledge of Venetian landmarks and history, and practical ability to handle the gondola. Successful candidates are granted a license and become a member of the Gondoliers Guild. A romantic trip on a gondola is part of the Venice experience for many tourists, but you will have to dig quite deep for the fare. A gondola can carry up to six people, and the prices are cheaper during the day than the evening. There is a hefty tariff for the first 50 minutes and longer journeys rise in price every 20 minutes. There are plenty of stands (*stazi*) throughout the city, e.g. Riva del Carbon (near the Rialto Bridge), Bacino Orseolo (north-west of Piazza San Marco), at the railway station, and at the Hotel Danieli.

On foot during the floods
Flooding (*acqua alta*) occurs regularly in Venice between fall and April. The Venetians seem to have got used to it, but it is a nuisance for tourists. As St Mark's Square is the city's lowest point, the flooding starts there. Affected squares and streets are provided with duckboards (*passarelle*) that allow pedestrians to keep their feet dry, and many *vaporetto* stops have signs indicating dry routes and routes with duckboards. Visitors at this time of year might do as well to pack waterproof boots, although many of the hotels have large stocks of these and will happily lend them out to guests.
Water level information (recorded message):
Tel 199/16 51 65. www. commune.venezia.it/maree

Museums, music, and drama

Palazzo Mocenigo

Situated just off the Grand Canal, the palace was left to the city of Venice by its owner, the last of this branch of the Mocenigo family, in the mid-twentieth century. The *palazzo* (in fact, four *palazzi*) is decorated in an 18th-century style with many frescoes and paintings of the Mocenigo family. It has now been converted into a small museum in which visitors can view the state rooms on the first floor along with a collection of 18th-century costumes. Paintings of notable members of the Mocenigo family, as well as public figures such as King Charles II of England, line the walls. Interesting decorative features include stucco or frescoed ceilings and period furniture. If you are retracing the footsteps of Lord Byron, note that this is not the Palazzo Mocenigo that Byron stayed in; he lodged in another building belonging to the same family further down the Grand Canal.
Santa Croce 1992;
Tel 041/72 17 98;

Tradition that has grown over centuries: Campo Santo.

Apr–Oct Tues–Sun
10.00–17.00,
Nov–Mar 10.00–16.00.
www.museicivicineveneziani.it

Casa di Carlo Goldoni

The Gothic Palazzo Centanni-Goldoni, the playwright's birth house, exhibits mementos of this author of typical Venetian comedies (see p. 82).
San Polo 2794;
Tel 041/275 93 25;
Apr–Oct Thurs–Tues
10.00–17.00,
Nov–Mar 10.00–16.00,
closed 1 Jan, 1 May, 25 Dec.
www. museicivicineveneziani.it

Shopping

Aliani

An absolute must for all lovers of fine Italian food. This store stocks the finest delicatessen, such as ham, salami, cheeses, and a good selection of wines.
Ruga Vecchia di San
Giovanni, San Polo 654;
Tel 041/522 49 13

Cenerentola

In 1989 Lidiana Vallongo revived an old tradition of embroidering gold and silver thread, beads, and sequins onto handmade lampshades.

Each piece is a one-off, and the quality of the work can be viewed by lamplight.
Calle dei Saoneri,
San Polo 2718;
Tel 041/523 20 06.
www.cenerentola.net

Color Casa

Only the best quality fabric is available here, with creations in satin and silk, as well as ties, handkerchiefs, cushion covers, and bags.
San Polo 1989–1991;
Tel 041/523 60 71.
www.colorcasavenezia.it

Il Nido delle Cicogne

The "stork's nest" stocks chic clothing and accessories with real style and polish for the very smallest members of the family.
Campo San Tomà, San Polo
2806; Tel 041/528 74 97.

Mascari

This artisan and store owner sells everything connected with Venetian boats – how about a model gondola, or a kit? There are also plenty of picture books and specialist literature on the long tradition of gondola building.
Calle Secondo dei Saoneri,
San Polo 2680;
Tel 041/71 93 72.
www.veniceboats.com

Gilberto Penzo

This artisan and store owner sells everything connected with Venetian boats – how about a model gondola, or a kit? There are also plenty of picture books and specialist literature on the long tradition of gondola building.
Calle Secondo dei Saoneri,
San Polo 2680,
Tel 041/71 93 72,
www.veniceboats.com

Il Baule Blu

Shopping heaven for teddy bear fans. Some of the bears are handmade, others growl or play a tune if you press them. If your teddy has been injured you are also in the right place, as indicated by the "Teddy Hospital" sign at the entrance. The store also stocks other stuffed animals and small accessories.
Campo San Tomà,
San Polo 2916 a;
Tel 041/71 94 48.

Lombardi

Silverware of every description and price in two shops next door to one another (both part of the same firm). Many of the useful and decorative utensils are made in Venice according to the long-standing local tradition of silverware manufacture. How about a frame for your most beautiful photo of Venice?
Ponte di San Polo,
San Polo 2099/2100;
Tel 041/523 24 70.

Valeria Bellinaso

When the sun beats down in the middle of summer you really need something on your head, and this store stocks attractive sun hats, although they are not exactly cheap. Properly attired, nothing stands between you and a romantic gondola trip. A scarf or a featherweight silk bag, also in stock here, would match nicely.
Campo Sant'Aponal,
San Polo 1226;
Tel 041/522 33 51.

Eating and drinking

Antica Birraria La Corte

Situated in an old brewery, this is a bar to be recom-

From left: "Venice's stomach": the fish is always fresh in the Pescheria, the neo-Gothic market building; Casa di Carlo Goldoni – inner courtyard and outdoor staircase; the lobby and terrace of the Santa Chiara Hotel.

These pages give additional information for the area described in the "Highlights" chapter (pp. 74–91).

mended. You can enjoy pizza, pasta, various grilled delicacies, or even horse meat inside in the courtyard or outside, if the weather's good.
Campo San Polo,
San Polo 2168;
Tel 041/275 05 70;
10.00–14.30, 19.00–22.30,
daily.

Antica Trattoria Poste Vecie
A fine *trattoria* and one of the city's oldest restaurants. Its proximity to the fish market guarantees fresh produce and the best fish and seafood dishes. You can sit in the dining room or out in the greenery of the garden and enjoy tasty dishes and good wine in a romantic atmosphere.
Pescheria, San Polo 1608;
Tel 041/721 822;
closed Tues.
www. postevecie.com

Cantina Do Mori
Venetians have been meeting up in this popular *bacaro* near the fish market since 1642, and nowadays tourists can too. There are all sorts of copper utensils hanging from the ceiling. A great selection of wines and tasty *tramezzini*, and an enjoyable and atmospheric time is guaranteed in extremely agreeable and charming surroundings.
Calle dei Do Mori,
San Polo 429;
Tel 041/522 54 01;
Mon–Sat 8.30–20.30.

Da Fiore
Mara and Maurizio Martin's gourmet restaurant has received a Michelin star and is often patronized by stars and celebrities. Imaginative and creative fish dishes, tasty risottos, a wide selection of

desserts and cheeses, and a select wine list make any visit a special occasion. It is very popular, despite the high prices, so a timely reservation is recommended, especially in peak season.
Calle del Scaleter,
San Polo 2202 a;
Tel 041/72 13 08;
Tues–Sat 12.20–14.20,
19.30–22.00.
www.dafiore.net

Gelateria Alaska
Carlo Pistacchi, a past master in his field, runs an ice-cream shop – or rather, ice bar – in this typical old Venetian street. His homemade varieties are a sensation – along with the usual ones, he has created all sorts of tempting exotic flavors, such as artichoke, celery, fennel, ginger, fig, and many more. The ice cream is, of course, freshly made from the best, organic ingredients.
Calle Larga dei Bari,
Santa Croce 1159;
Tel 041/71 52 11;
summer 10.00–12.00,
winter Tues–Sun
13.00–21.00.

La Zucca
If you enjoy vegetarian food or just fancy a change from all the fish offered in so many of Venice's restaurants, this place near the Rialto Bridge is for you. There's a good selection of creative vegetarian dishes and a few with meat, and if you're lucky you'll get one of the few seats by the canal with the best view.
Ponte del Megio,
Santa Croce 1762;
Tel 041/5 24 15 70;
Mon–Sat 12.30–14.30,
19.00–22.30.
www.lazucca.it

Accommodation

Ai Due Fanali
The church of San Simeone Profeta next door has been here since 967, once sharing a common prayer room for gardeners and fishermen with the hotel building. Often rebuilt over the centuries, the hotel has 16 modern rooms and is decorated with canvases by the 16th-century mannerist painter Jacopo Palma Il Giovane. There is a spectacular view over the Grand Canal and the rest of Venice from the roof terrace.
Santa Croce 946;
Tel 041/71 84 90.
www.aiduefanali.com

Al Sole
A hotel situated in a 16th-century *palazzo* in one of the most picturesque corners of town. Some of the guest rooms have venerable old furniture, but all have been refurbished. The adjoining garden is also atmospheric.
Fondamenta Minotto,
Santa Croce 134;
Tel 041/244 03 28.
www.alsolehotels.com

Casa Caburlotto
This church hostel run by nuns is the place for visitors looking for a reasonably priced place to stay. The garden is a lovely place to spend some time, and the rooms are clean and uncluttered. One downside: tthe doors close promptly at 22.30.
Fondamenta Rizzi,
Santa Croce 316;
Tel 041/71 08 77.

Guerrato
Value for money and good service in a former monastery. Some of the rooms have old

furniture. Another plus: step out of the hotel into the bustle of the Rialto market and Venice's highlights are but a stone's throw away.
Calle Drio la Scimia,
San Polo 240 a;
Tel 041/522 71 31.
www.pensioneguerrato.it

Locanda Sant'Agostin
Leonardo and Federico run a small, cozy hotel situated in a magnificent 16th-century *palazzo*. As you might expect, all the rooms are elegantly decorated and some are furnished with antiques. A leisurely breakfast in the dining room will help prepare you for sightseeing in the lively districts of San Polo and Santa Croce.
Campo Sant'Agostin,
San Polo 2344;
Tel 041/275 94 14. www.
locandasantagostin.com

Santa Chiara
A small hotel located right beside the bustling coach station in Piazzale Roma; despite its position it is actually very quiet.
Fondamenta Cassetti,
Santa Croce 548;
Tel 041/520 08 80.
www.hotelsantachiara.it

Nightlife

Il Nono Risorto
Jazz and blues fans come here for good music and drinks – and a decent pizza, which are good value for money. Sit outside in the garden in summer. Just a few minutes from the Rialto Bridge.
Sotoportego di Siora
Bettina, Santa Croce 2338;
Tel 041/524 11 69.

Museums, music, and drama

Centro d'Arte Contemporanea di Punta della Dogana

Contemporary art from the private collection of the entrepreneur and collector François Pinault is exhibited in a former customs house on the tip of Dorsoduro. The emphasis is on the large-format works and installations for which there is no room in the Palazzo Grassi, also run by the Pinault Collection. The internal design of the baroque building is the work of the Japanese architect Tadao Ando.
Punta della Dogana, Dorsoduro 2;
Palazzo Grassi information:
Tel 199/13 91 39.
www.palazzograssi.it

Giorgio Cini Foundation

Housed in the former monastery of San Giorgio Maggiore, this institute exhibits an extensive collection of valuable paintings, etchings, Gobelin work, porcelain, furniture, and musical instruments. The adjoining

Teatro Verde open-air stage hosts various drama and dance performances.
Fondazione Giorgio Cini, Isola di San Giorgio Maggiore;
Tel 041/271 02 80;
Tues–Sun 10.00–18.00.
www.cini.it

Teatro a L'Avogaria

A small stage focusing on the city's rich dramatic tradition, such as Carlo Goldoni's comedies, which were premiered here. The company also has some experimental drama in its repertoire.
Corte Zappa, Dorsoduro 1617;
Tel 041/520 61 30.
www.teatroavogaria.it

Festivals and events

Festa del Redentore

This festival commemorates the devastating plague epidemic of 1576; pretty much every boat in the city is decorated with lights and flowers and assembles on the Giudecca Canal the evening before the festival to wait for the fireworks at midnight. There are celebrations on

land as well, of course. On Sunday there is a procession from the Zattere across the Giudecca Canal to the Church of the Redeemer, Il Redentore.
3rd Sun in Jul, party and fireworks followed by illuminated boat procession.

Sport and leisure

Canottieri Giudecca

For a few Euros, non-members can train in *voga alla Veneta* (Venetian-style rowing) alongside expert rowers at one of the most active rowing clubs in Venice.
Fondamenta a Fianco del Ponte Lungo;
Tel 041/58 74 09; office hours: Tues and Thurs 16.00–18.00. www. canottierigiudecca.com

Piscina Communale

Venice is not a place to go for beaches and swimming, though there is the Lido. But if you really feel the need to cool down, try this popular municipal pool on the western tip of the Giudecca, with restricted bathing times because of the crowds.
Sacca Fisola 82;
Tel 041/528 54 30;
closed mid-Jun–end Aug.

Shopping

Arras

A store run by the Laguna cooperative selling a good selection of nice, handwoven fabric, shirts, jackets, trousers, and other textiles. Brightly hued items made from silk, wool, and cotton.
Campiello Squellini, Dorsoduro 3235/3236;
Tel 041/522 64 60;
Mon–Sat 9.00–13.00, 15.30–19.30.

Billa

Anyone strolling through Venice will soon notice that although there are plenty of small boutiques, there are practically no supermarkets. And then you find one in Dorsoduro! It is open seven days a week and sells bread, wine, fruit, and vegetables as well as cheese and cold meats.
Zattere, Dorsoduro 1491;
Tel 041/522 61 87;
9.00–20.00, daily.

Il Melograno

If you want to indulge your body, this natural cosmetics store has a wide selection of soaps, lotions, potions, and creams. A mixture of scents – and the friendly staff – greet you as you enter.
Campo Santa Margherita, Dorsoduro 2999;
Tel 041/528 51 17.

Signor Blum

The proprietor of this shop, Signor Blum, has been making objects out of wood in his workshop since 1978. One of his amazing, three-dimensional wooden puzzles would make a great souvenir or present.
Campo San Barnaba, Dorsoduro 2840;
Tel 041/522 72 12.
www.signorblum.com

Eating and drinking

Ai Gondolieri

A restaurant for gourmets located right next to the Guggenheim museum and one of the best in Venice, spoiling its customers with dishes cooked with ingredients that vary by season and region, such as truffles from Alba. Helpful service and a warm atmosphere in the little

Festa del Redentore: fascinating façade projections.

From left: San Nicolò dei Mendicoli in Dorsoduro is an architectural jewel; the highlights of the Festa del Redentore are the fireworks and the boats decorated with flowers; fresh cappuccino is always popular.

DORSODURO, LA GIUDECCA, AND SAN GIORGIO MAGGIORE

These pages give additional information for the area described in the "Highlights" chapter (pp. 92–111).

dining rooms, although all this comes at a price.
San Vio, Dorsoduro 366;
Tel 041/528 63 96;
closed Tues.
www.aigondolieri.com

Alla Palanca

A short *vaporetto* trip to the island of La Giudecca will take you to the best homemade food, and you'll be joining crowds of locals who also enjoy the traditional dishes served here. Try spaghetti with mixed seafood or choose from the grilled fish, which is always fresh. Good value for money.
Fondamenta Sant'Eufemia, Giudecca 448; Tel 041/528 7719; closed Sun.

Altanella

Good fish dishes are the order of the day here. The best seats are on a wooden terrace right beside the canal. There are not many tables so booking ahead is advisable.
Calle delle Erbe,
Giudecca 268;
Tel 041/5 22 77 80;
closed Mon and Tues.

Antica Trattoria La Furatole

Massimiliano Peltrera will bring excellent *fritto misto* and other fish and seafood delicacies from the lagoon to your table. Add a well-cooled white wine from the Veneto and the epicurean experience is complete; a real gourmet tip for Venetians.
Calle Lunga S. Bamba,
Dorsoduro 2869 a;
Tel 041/520 85 94

Do Mori

Do Mori (the name means "two Moors") was founded by ex-employees of Harry's Bar. The emphasis is on Vene-

tian cuisine, particularly fish. The view of the canal is really beautiful and the prices are not that bad, for Venice.
Sant'Eufemia,
Giudecca 588;
Tel 041/522 54 01;
closed Sun.

Harry's Dolci

The famous (and not quite so pricey) daughter concern of Harry's Bar at the Sant'-Eufemia *vaporetto* stop; worth a visit in summer. Delicious cakes, sweet confectionery, and also more substantial dishes and snacks. The range and selection is just right for a rest on the wonderful terrace.
Fondamenta San Biagio,
Giudecca 773;
Tel 041/522 48 44;
summer Apr–Oct,
closed Tues.
www.cipriani.com

Accommodation

Ca' Pisani

This hotel was opened in the year 2000, in what could be called the artistic heart of the city. The rooms in this Renaissance palace are elegantly furnished with pieces from the 1930s and 1940s. Pictures by the painter, Fortunato Depero, an Italian futurist, and other works of art are distributed throughout the hotel.
Rio Terra Antonio Foscarini,
Dorsoduro 979 a;
Tel 041/240 14 11.
www.capisanihotel.it

Cipriani

The hotel opened in 1963 and has since become one of the best, and most expensive, places to stay on the lagoon. The epitome of luxury and beauty (or perhaps deca-

dence?) with garden views over the lagoon, visitors soon forget the bustle of St Mark's Square when staying here. There are delights for the palate both on the terrace and in the restaurant. There are even chauffeur-driven water taxis and a private marina for guests who arrive by yacht.
Giudecca 10;
Tel 041/520 77 44.
www.hotelcipriani.it

Pensione Accademia

Guests are welcomed to the 17th-century Villa Maravege with a historic atmosphere, beautiful antique furniture, and absolute peace. It was used as the Russian Consulate until the 1930s. Katherine Hepburn's character in the 1955 film *Summertime* is supposed to have lived here. The villa is situated in two wonderful flower gardens, which guests can use.
Fondamenta Bollani,
Dorsoduro 1058;
Tel 041/521 01 88.
www.pensioneaccademia.it

Nightlife

Café Noir

An internet café and hip meeting place for young Venetians and even tourists. Often so full that people have to hang out in the street in front of the bar.
Calle dei Preti,
Dorsoduro 3805;
Tel 041/71 63 49; 19.00–2.00,
closed Sun.

Cinema Accademia

A cinema for fans of classic films, although with many relatively current movies in its schedule. Every so often there will be a special showing of

the original version of an English-language production.
Accademia,
Dorsoduro 1019;
Tel 041/528 77 06.

Da Codroma

A well-known *osteria*, for decades popular with students, whose old-fashioned rooms host live gigs on certain days, from blues to folk from all over the world.
Fondamenta Briati,
Dorsoduro 2540;
Tel 041/524 67 89;
19.00–1.00,
closed Sun and Mon.

Margaret Duchamp

A young and generally smart crowd meet here in the evenings to listen to the house band. The atmosphere is restrained and of course cool, although in summer patrons move out onto the Campo in front of the bar. Only very few bars in Venice are open as late as this.
Campo Santa Margherita,
Dorsoduro 3019;
Tel 041/528 62 55;
20.00–2.00, closed Tues.

Venice Jazz Club

Internationally renowned jazz artists and ensembles play four concerts a week here. The Venice Jazz Club quartet includes some of the finest Italian musicians who are often joined by special guests. They play modern compositions and revisit the standards, as well as play special "tributes to" legends such as Miles Davis and Duke Ellington. One or two drinks are usually included in the price of admission.
Fondamenta del Squero,
Dorsoduro 3102.
www.venicejazzclub.com

Museums, music, and drama

Teatro Fondamenta Nuove
A small but active company staging mostly avant-garde pieces in Italian. There are puppet shows for younger audiences.
Cannaregio 5013;
Tel 041/522 44 98.
www.teatrofondamentanuo ve.it

Palazzo Labia
Dating from the 17th–18th centuries, this baroque gem is off the normal tourist trail but well worth a visit. Originally owned by the Labia family, the building fell into disrepair in the 19th century, but by the 1950s a change of ownership had revived its fortunes. A masquerade ball held here was one of the most lavish social events of the 20th century and launched the career of fashion designer Pierre Cardin. Cecil Beaton's photographs of the ball recorded the event. Concerts are regularly held in this *palazzo*, which has frescoes by Tiepolo and belongs to the Italian broadcasting company. It also has a conference center.

Campo S. Geremia 275;
Tel 041/524 28 12.
www.palazzolabia.it

Teatro Malibran
The name of the theater is taken from Maria Malibran (1808–1836), a great Spanish-French mezzo soprano and the most famous *prima donna* of her time. Originally known as the Teatro di San Giovanni Crisostomo, the theater has been in existence since the 17th century and is considered the most beautiful opera house for miles around. The current appearance of the building dates from the 19th century, although extensive refurbishment has recently been undertaken.
Campiello Malibran 5873.
www.italianticketoffice.it

Sport and leisure

Casino di Venezia
This elegant casino is housed in the splendid Palazzo Vendramin-Calergi, located right beside the canal. Visitors can pay a simple admission charge or pay a slightly higher price which includes some gambling choices. Jacket and tie required.

Tel 041/529 71 11;
Sun–Thurs 14.45–2.30,
Fri–Sat 14.45–3.00.
www.casinovenezia.it

Shopping

Bianconero
A store housing a photo archive of famous and rare photographs of famous people in Venice. Particularly good for browsing.
Salizzada del Pistór,
Cannaregio 4460;
Tel 041/522 87 81;
Tues–Sat 10.00–13.00,
15.30–19.30.

Coin
Despite the high rents, overcrowding, and long tradition of small boutiques in Venice, there is one department store offering an alternative to the pricey selections in the stores in the area. In principle, they stock everything, ranging from clothing to household utensils and domestic goods, though with an eye to sleek design – this is Venice, after all. This is the Venice branch of one of Italy's largest department store chains.
Fontego Salizzada San Crisostomo, Cannaregio 5787; Tel 041/520 35 81.

Giacomo Rizzo
Not far from the Coin department store, this is a good place to buy typically Italian souvenirs. And what could be more Italian than pasta? Giacomo Rizzo is a pasta manufacturer who, for the past four generations, has been selling pasta in all kinds of shapes and sizes, including hats and gondolas, and it's all beautifully packaged, making it the perfect gift for friends and relatives back home.

Calle San Giovanni Crisostomo, Cannaregio 5778;
Tel 041/522 28 24;
Thurs–Tues 8.30–13.00,
15.20–19.30.

Eating and drinking

Anice Stellato
A simple bar which is family-run. Many locals call in here, which is perhaps indicative of the quality of the food and the good atmosphere. Spices are used imaginatively in the kitchen, as the name ("star anise") might suggest.
Fondamenta della Sensa, Cannaregio 3272;
Tel 041/72 07 44;
closed Mon and Tues.

Brek
Part of a chain of restaurants offering quality food at "normal" prices. You can inspect the food at your leisure at various counters and then compile your meal. A good alternative to Venice's generally very pricey restaurants.
Lista di Spagna, Cannaregio 124;
Tel 041/244 01 58;
closed Mon.

Gam-Gam
After visiting the Ghetto district you can experience Jewish and international cuisine at this kosher bar. How about some *Antipasti Israeliani* as a starter or some falafel, typical Middle Eastern cuisine?
Sotoportego del Ghetto Vecchio, Cannaregio 1122;
Tel 041/71 52 84;
closed Fri evening and Sat.

Melograno
This restaurant belonging to the Hesperia Hotel, offers both regional specialties and

The casino is to be found in an early Renaissance palace.

From left: Life on the water – a canalside house entrance; the imposing appearance of the Scuola Nuova in the Misericordia district of Cannaregio; cocktail break; impressions of Venice from a stroll through the city.

CANNAREGIO

These pages give additional information for the area described in the "Highlights" chapter (pp. 112–127).

one or two epicurean delights at a reasonable price.
Campiello Riello, Cannaregio 459; Tel 041/71 52 51.

Mirai
Another take on fish: this Japanese restaurant is an alternative for those wanting a change from Venetian cuisine. Japanese visitors, foreign tourists, and even locals come for the sushi, different varieties of which are made fresh each day here.
Lista di Spagna, Cannaregio 227; Tel 041/220 65 17; evenings only, closed Mon.

Accommodation

Abbazia
You rarely find beautiful hotels near stations, but this hotel, once an abbey, is one. Refurbishment has retained much of the old monastery buildings, such as the refectory with its chancel, which is used as a lounge. The rooms are modern and the garden is pure luxury for Venice.
Calle Priuli dei Cavaletti, Cannaregio 66/68; Tel 041/71 73 33. www.abbaziahotel.com

Al Vagon
This centrally located, family-run hotel is within easy reach of St Mark's Square. It offers good value for money and a few of the simple rooms have a view of the Grand Canal, while the others look out onto the surrounding streets. The restaurant in the hotel serves superb Venetian dishes and has a typical Venetian covered terrace where you can sit in the shade in summer and watch the gondolas.

Campiello Riccardo Selvatico, Cannaregio 5619; Tel 041/528 56 26. www.hotelalvagon.com

Amadeus
A centrally located four-star hotel, offering good service and comfort. The lobby and the rooms are decorated with different elements drawn from the various periods of Venetian history. Guests love the green garden in summer.
Lista di Spagna, Cannaregio 227; Tel 041/220 60 00. www.hotelamadeusvenice.it

Ca' Pozzo
Cunningly combining a Venetian hotel with elements of modern design and a good location make this three-star hotel a real insider tip. The modern rooms are well turned out and breakfast is served in a leisurely fashion in the hotel's little courtyard.
Sotoportego Ca' Pozzo, Cannaregio 1279; Tel 041/524 05 04. www.capozzovenice.com

Casa Cardinal Piazza
This church-run hostel in Palazzo Contarini-Minelli is good news for visitors to Venice on tighter budgets, and the simple rooms all have a bathroom. Visitors who wish to make a night of it are possibly better off elsewhere, however, as the doors close at about 23.00.
Fondamenta Gasparo Contarini, Cannaregio 3539 a; Tel 041/72 13 88.

Al Ponte Antico
Visitors wishing to stay right in the heart of St Mark's should book early to get one

of the new rooms. Four of these even have a view of the Grand Canal and the Rialto Bridge. Teatro Malibran just around the corner is worth a visit. Housed in a fine 16th-century building, there is a terrace where you can dine on warm evenings.
Calle dell'Aseo, Cannaregio 5768; Tel 041/241 19 44. www.alponteantico.com

Grand Hotel Palazzo dei Dogi
This luxurious hotel, housed in an old monastery with a large garden, offers every comfort. The rooms either overlook the canal or the lagoon. A motorboat shuttle to St Mark's and the Rialto is all part of the service. An excellent restaurant, and an attractive spa and gym at the Club H2O.
Fondamenta Madonna dell'Orto, Cannaregio 3500; Tel 041/220 81 81. www.boscolohotels.com

Ostello
Young people, students, and the price-conscious will find this a reasonable and central place to stay, ten minutes away from the Rialto Bridge and 15 minutes from St Mark's Square. The view from the garden is of the church of Santa Fosca.
Cannaregio 2372; Tel 041/715 775; open every day except Christmas. www.santafosca.it

Nightlife

Casanova
There's not a club scene in Venice like the one on the Adriatic coast, but Casanova,

near the station, is an internet café during the day and a disco in the evenings.
Lista di Spagna, Cannaregio 158 a; Tel 041/275 01 99; internet café from 9.00, disco until 3.00.

Cinema Giorgione
Giorgione Movie D'Essai is one of the city's few cinemas. Various screens show foreign productions (often in the original English or French with Italian subtitles).
Rio Terra dei Franceschi, Santi Apostoli, Cannaregio 4612; Tel 041/522 62 98.

Iguana
A lively Tex-Mex restaurant that attracts a young crowd and night owls from the party zone of Fondamenta della Misericordia. Happy hour is from 18.00 to 19.00 if you want to spare your wallet.
Fondamenta della Misericordia, Cannaregio 2515; Tel 041/71 35 61; 18.00–2.00, closed Mon.

The Fiddler's Elbow Irish Pub
If you can't do without Guinness even on holiday, you'll find an Irish atmosphere and live music here. Patrons can sit outside in the summer. Popular with Venetians, tourists, and ex-pats alike, there's a big screen for sporting events. And if you like it here, and are on the modern equivalent of the Grand Tour, there are also branches in Rome and Florence.
Campiello Testori/Strada Nova, Cannaregio 3847; Tel 041/523 99 30; 17.00–0.30.

Museums, music, and drama

Museo Diocesano

The Diocesan Museum is housed in the cloister of the monastery of Sant'Apollonia and has a wealth of liturgical apparatus and Mass vestments. Sculpture and paintings by mostly Venetian artists, but also modern religious art.
Sant'Apollonia,
Castello 4312;
Tel 041/522 91 66;
10.00–18.00, daily. www.
museodiocesanovenezia.it

Museo Storico Navale and Padiglioni delle Navi

This museum of maritime history is situated where the Rio dell'Arsenale flows into St Mark's Canal and houses a collection of various model ships, weapons, and nautical apparatus illustrating Venice's long seafaring traditions, as well as exhibits from Italy's maritime history. A visit to the Padiglioni delle Navi on the Fondamenta della Madonna is also included in the admission price.

Riva San Biagio,
Castello 2148;
Tel 041/520 02 76;
Mon–Fri 8.45–13.30,
Sat 8.45–13.00, closed Sun.

Museo Querini-Stampalia

The interior of Palazzo Querini-Stampalia has been refurbished as an exhibition space by Carlo Scarpa and Mario Botta, and houses a major collection of precious paintings and furniture, musical instruments, and chinaware, all giving an insight into Venetian baroque culture. Paintings by Bellini and Tiepolo and a collection of genre paintings by Pietro Longhi are worthy of special attention (see p. 134).
Campiello Querini,
Castello 4778;
Tel 041/522 52 35;
Tues–Sat 10.00–20.00,
Sun 10.00–19.00.
www.querinistampalia.it

Festivals and events

Biennale Internazionale d'Arte

The art fair is held in the exhibition space in the district of Castello during "odd" years, introducing aspiring new artists and reappraising the well known. Along with the various contemporary pieces, the often avant-garde national pavilions are worth seeing on their own. The accompanying events held all over the city have established the fair in the city's events calendar (see p. 142).
Giardini Pubblici
1st week in Jun–end Oct
or beginning of Nov;
Tel 041/521 87 11.
www.labiennale.org,
www.labiennaledivenezia.it

Festa di San Pietro di Castello

A big festival held around the church of San Pietro di Castello, the seat of the Patriarch of Venice, with performances and concerts, and snack stands to fortify the inner being.
Last weekend in Jun.

Sport and leisure

Giardini Pubblici

Venice's most extensive park area with lots of greenery, shady spots with benches, and play areas for the children. The national pavilions for the Biennale Internazionale d'Arte, an important and prestigious exhibition of contemporary art (see photograph left), are also set up here.
Viale dei Giardini Pubblici.

Stadio Pier Luigi Pensa

As a rule you can obtain tickets for home fixtures at SSC Venezia (formerly AC Venezia) on match day without a problem. However, since its foundation in 1907, the team has rarely played in Serie A, the top Italian league, and even then has made little impact.
Sant'Elena;
Tel 041/520 68 99.
www.veneziacalcio.it

Shopping

Barbieri

Elegant and chic gentlemen's and ladies' Italian fashion, with acceptable prices.
Calle della Madonna,
Castello 3403;
Tel 041/522 81;
Mon–Sat 10.00–12.30,
15.30–19.30.

Ca' del Sol

Venetian carnival masks, handmade to historical patterns, and brightly painted new creations as well as beautiful costumes are all presented here in some very stylish surroundings. You can browse, make your choices and try things on at your leisure to a musical accompaniment, and those who so wish can take a look at the nearby artists' workshop.
Fondamenta dell'Osmarin,
Castello 4964;
Tel 041/528 55 49;
9.30–19.30, daily.
www.cadelsolmaschere.com

Didovich

A popular confectioner's in Campo Santa Marina and one of the best in the city. The almost irresistible scent of baking greets you as soon as you enter this *pasticceria* and the Austrian-style apple strudel (*strudel di mele*) is sinfully good.
Campo Santa Marina,
Castello 5908;
Tel 041/523 00 17;
Mon–Sat 6.30–20.00,
closed Sun.

The Biennale Internazionale d'Arte is held in the grounds of the Giardini Pubblici.

From left: The Arsenale, Venice's weapons chest; the tomb of Pietro Mocenigo in the Basilica dei Santi Giovanni e Paolo; the cloister of Sant'Apollonia – the Museo Diocesano; Venetian atmosphere: Hostaria da Franz.

These pages give additional information for the area described in the "Highlights" chapter (pp. 128–143).

Kalimala

There is a long tradition of leatherworking in Venice. This store stocks leather handbags, shoulder bags, and backpacks of all shapes and hues.
Salizzada San Lio, Castello 5387; Tel 041/528 35 96; 9.30–19.30, daily.

Vino e Vini

You can hardly miss this wine emporium – there are vine leaves growing over the entrance! A good selection of decent wines from the Veneto, including keenly priced *vino da tavola*. There is a wide selection of grappa for those who prefer something a little stronger.
Fondamenta dei Furlani, Castello 3301; Tel 041/521 01 84; 9.00–13.00, 17.00–20.00, daily.

Eating and drinking

Birreria Forst

A good place for a quick drink and a little snack, or even for an aperitif. The *tramezzini* here taste particularly good washed down with a beer.
Calle delle Rasse, Castello 4540; Tel 041/523 05 57.

Corte Sconta

Unfortunately, the word is already out on Marco Proietto's excellent fish restaurant; you should plan on booking a few days in advance, but the quality of the food more than makes up for this. Try the fresh antipasti, homemade noodles, and various fish dishes. As the restaurant is very popular, it can sometimes get a bit loud.

Calle del Pestrin, Castello 3886; Tel 041/522 70 24; closed Sun and Mon.

Dai Tosi

A recommended *trattoria* near the Biennale grounds, rarely frequented by tourists (but for how much longer?).
Seco Marina, Castello 738; Tel 041/523 71 02; closed Wed.

Hostaria da Franz

Small but perfectly formed and also near the Biennale grounds in the Giardini Pubblici, this is the place to try excellent seafood, some of which even comes from the waters of the lagoon. In good weather, the seats on the little terrace have a real Venetian atmosphere.
Fondamenta San Giuseppe, Castello 754; Tel 041/522 08 61.
www.hostariadafranz.com

Accommodation

Danieli

This hotel is situated in three Venetian houses from the 14th, 19th, and 20th centuries, and there is elegance and luxury wherever you look: marble, chandeliers, silk wallpaper, Persian carpets, and a magnificent Gothic staircase are all part of the rich trappings. The hotel's immediate proximity to St Mark's Square is also a plus point. The 1948 extension is not quite as impressive, but has a gourmet restaurant on its roof terrace with a magnificent view across the lagoon to the Lido. It is little wonder that this hotel is considered one of the most beautiful, and is certainly one of the most expensive, in the world.
Riva degli Schiavoni, Castello 4196; Tel 041/522 64 80. www. danieli.hotelinvenice.com

Locanda Silva

Five minutes' walk from St Mark's Square, this family-friendly hotel with its clean rooms has been run by the Ettore family since 1956. Value for money for Venice.
Fondamenta del Rimedio, Castello 5523; Tel 041/522 76 43.
www.locandasilva.it

Londra Palace

This luxury hotel, right next to the Biennale and on the best spot on the canal promenade near St Mark's, cleverly combines antiques and modern design. Tchaikovsky composed the first three movements of his Fourth Symphony during a stay here, and Italian lyrical poet Gabriele D'Annunzio was also a guest when he attended the unveiling of the equestrian statue of Victor Emanuel II nearby.
Riva degli Schiavoni, Castello 4171; Tel 041/520 05 33.
www.hotelondra.it

Metropole

A palazzo full of antiques, with plenty of luxury and a fine collection of musical instruments. Try to reserve a room with a lagoon view, it's worth it. There is a lunch buffet in the adjoining restaurant and a set menu in the evenings.
Riva degli Schiavoni, Castello 4149; Tel 041/520 50 44.
www.hotelmetropole.com

Palazzo Soderini

A reasonable place to stay on the beautiful Campo Bandiera e Moro, with simple, clean, modern rooms and a small garden. There is no intrusive signage on the *palazzo*, just a simple doorbell.
Campo Bandiera e Moro, Castello 3611; Tel 041/296 08 23.
www.palazzosoderini.it

Pensione Wildner

Everything is right in this simple hotel, from the prices to its location next to the lagoon. Many regular guests have discovered this for themselves, so book ahead.
Riva degli Schiavoni, Castello 4161; Tel 041/522 74 63.

Scandinavia

Housed in a building dating back 1,000 years, the walls and foundations of this comfortable hotel are from the Byzantine era. Located on the romantic Santa Maria Formosa Square, it offers views across the square and its beautiful church.
Campo Santa Maria Formosa, Castello 5340; Tel 041/522 35 07.
www.scandinaviahotel.com

Nightlife

L'Olandese Volante

Young people, especially students, meet here to drink beer, but "the Flying Dutchman" also serves little snacks and salads. In summer, a lucky few find a seat on the terrace.
Campo San Lio, Castello 5658; Tel 041/528 93 49; Mon–Thurs 11.00–0.30, Fri–Sat 11.00–2.00, Sun 17.00–0.30.

Museums, music, and drama

Villa Foscari (La Malcontenta)

Built with a classical pillared portico by Andrea Palladio between 1549 and 1563, this noble residence with agricultural land was the first great villa on the Brenta Canal and is still in the possession of the Foscari family. The great hall inside is captivating and the beautiful frescoes were executed by Giovanni Battista Zelotti and Battista Franco in the style of Paolo Veronese.
Via dei Turisti 9,
Malcontenta di Mira;
Tel 041/547 00 12;
Apr–Oct Tues and Sat
9.00–12.00.
www.lamalcontenta.com

Villa Pisani

The largest and most famous of the villas on the Brenta Canal is state-owned. Constructed in 1720 in beautiful grounds, the interior of this magnificent building still retains many of the original 18th-century features. The ballroom, with its fresco by Tiepolo, *The Glory of the Pisani Family*, makes a spec-

tacular setting for large art exhibitions.
Via Doge Pisani 7, Stra;
Tel 041/50 20 74; Apr–Sept
Tues–Sun 9.00–20.00,
Oct 9.00–18.00, Nov–Mar
9.00–17.00, closed 1 Jan, 1
May, 25 Dec. www.
villapisani.beniculturali.it

Festivals and events

Capodanno in Spiaggia

Those wishing to see in the New Year on the beach can join their friends on the Lido for hot drinks and snacks.
1 Jan.

Vogalonga

A big rowing regatta over a distance of some 30 km (19 miles) from St Mark's across the lagoon to the islands and back, ending at the Grand Canal. The festival was started in 1975 by a group of friends who wanted to put rowing back on the map in Venice, in the face of the increasing use of distinctly eco-unfriendly motorboats and their contribution to the deterioration of the city's buildings. It is a non-competitive event for amateurs.
A Sun in May

Festa della Sensa

This procession of historic boats from San Marco to the Lido is a tradition of great symbolic importance: the importance of the Adriatic, indeed of the sea in general, to Venice used to be marked by the doge on Ascension Day, when he would throw a ring into the water from his ceremonial boat, the *Bucintoro*, as a sign of the city's marriage to the Adriatic. Nowadays, the upper echelons of the church, the city, and the military travel across to the Lido, where the mayor carries out the tradition, throwing a ring and a wreath into the sea. This is followed by a Mass in the church of San Nicolò and the inevitable regatta.
Sun after Ascension.

International Film Festival

Cinema productions from all over the world compete for the Golden Lion at the Mostra Internazionale d'Arte Cinematografica. The importance of the film industry and a galaxy of stars of varying magnitude ensure lots of press attention. The movies in the official competition are screened in the Palazzo del Cinema on the Lido, although many of the city's open-air cinemas and movie theaters schedule a wider choice as part of the event.
Palazzo del Cinema;
Tel 041/521 88 57;
end Aug/beginning Sept.
www.labiennale.org

Fish Festival

A cheerful festival on the island of Burano, also known as "Fishermen's Island", which marks the importance of the sea to Venice. Stalls are

set up among the houses on the narrow streets selling fish (of course) and wine. A cheap way to have lunch "on the hoof" and a chance to see a Venetian festival in full swing.
3rd Sun in Sept.

Venice Marathon

Like any city worth its salt, Venice has its own marathon, which starts from the Villa Pisani in Stra, near Padua. The route follows level ground along the Brenta Canal to the finish line in St Mark's Square.
Usually on 4th Sun or
at end of Oct.
www.venicemarathon.it

Wine Festival

The tiny island of Sant'Erasmo is the scene of this beautiful festival in the fall. There are tasty snacks and good wines, of course, as well as music and the obligatory regatta.
1st Sun in Oct.

Sport and leisure

Circolo Golf Venezia

This verdant 18-hole golf course in Alberoni, the southern part of the Lido, must rank as one of the best in the world; its location between the lagoon and the sea is unforgettable. The course is playable throughout the year.
Lido di Venezia,
Strada Vecchia 1;
Tel 041/73 13 33; advance
reservations by telephone
recommended.
www.circologolfvenezia.it

Tennis Club Venezia

Non-members can book a court for a match here. This club on the Lido is one of the oldest tennis clubs in the world.

Marriage with the Sea: the Festa della Sensa.

From left: An amphibious habitat – it is easy to explore the lagoon by boat, as here from the island of Pellestrina; fishing boats in Chioggia; the Villa Pisani on the Riviera del Brenta; Murano glassblowers in action.

These pages give additional information for the area described in the "Highlights" chapter (pp. 144–161).

Lido di Venezia, Lungomare Guglielmo Marconi 41 d;
Tel 041/526 03 35; advance reservations by telephone recommended.

Lido di Jesolo
Anyone wanting to lounge on a sandy beach without having to pay for the privilege will have to reconcile themselves to an hour's journey to the north-east of the lagoon. There is a bus route and a ferry connection in the summer months.
Lido di Jesolo.
www.jesolo.it

Caroman Oasis
This nature reserve of 40 ha (100 acres) has dunes that are home to rare plants and animals, especially birds such as the Kentish plover and the little tern. There are marked paths through the reserve.
Pellestrina, Caroman Oasis.
www.pellestrina.it

Shopping

Barovier & Toso
On the "glassblower's quay" there are still several workshops dedicated to this traditional handicraft. Extremely precious and creative products available for a price are produced by the following firm, for example.
Fondamenta dei Vetrai 28, Murano;
Tel 041/73 90 49.
www.barovier.com

La Murrina
A company founded in 1968 in cooperation with several designers, using old glassblowing techniques to produce classic and contemporary ornaments and glassware, especially lamps.

Fondamenta Riva Longa 17, Murano;
Tel 041/527 46 05.
www.lamurrina.com

Pasticceria Cioccolateria Pettenò
Mestre, jammed with traffic and thus of little interest to tourists, is also home to this cioccolateria, a delight for the eyes and palates of lovers of Venetian confectionery. Candied fruit coated in the finest light, dark, and full milk chocolate, all sorts of sophisticated pralines, nougat, and many other delicious delicacies are sold here. The store supplies high-quality products to numerous cafés in the area and in Venice.
Via Vallon 1, Carpenedo di Mestre;
Tel 041/534 06 73.

Vetreria Artistica Archimede Seguso S.r.l.
A great selection of fine glassware to choose from. This workshop, once run by the master glassblower, Archimede Seguso, specializes in gift items, lamps, and especially chandeliers.
Fondamenta Serenella 18, Murano;
Tel 041/73 90 48;
9.00–19.30, daily.
www.aseguso.com

Eating and drinking

Ca' Vignotto
The island of Sant'Erasmo is considered Venice's kitchen garden, and fruit and vegetables from here are sold all over the city. Visitors to the island who stray into this restaurant are in for a surprise. There is no menu, but what reaches the table is healthy portions of reason-

ably priced, good food. Word has naturally got around, with the result that advance reservations are recommended, especially on summer weekends.
Via Forti 71, Sant'Erasmo;
Tel 041/244 40 00;
closed Tues.

Osteria al Ponte del Diavolo
Situated on the road from the vaporetto stop to Torcello cathedral, this osteria, serving freshly prepared fish dishes to eat, with a glass of wine on a shady terrace, has made a name for itself with tourists and locals alike.
Torcello 29;
Tel 041/73 04 01.

Ristorante Dalla Mora
The cooking is good and fairly priced, and the service friendly. A good place to pop into when exploring Murano.
Fondamenta Manin 75, Murano;
Tel 041/527 46 06.

Accommodation

Des Bains
A Belle Époque luxury hotel chosen by Luchino Visconti to feature in his film adaptation of the Thomas Mann novella, Death in Venice. The hotel has beautiful grounds and its own wooden bathing huts on the beach. The excellent Liberty Restaurant offers guests selected, exquisitely prepared dishes, and a selection of rather pleasant wines.
Lungomare Marconi 17, Lido; Tel 041/526 59 21.

Excelsior
This five-star hotel is a little slice of paradise, with a magnificent view of the canals

and the city; no wonder it has come to rank amongst the finest in Europe. It still has something of the turn of the 20th century about it, when the upper classes would spend their summers on the Adriatic. The modern hotel has a Spanish or Moorish feel to it, especially the inner courtyard. Whether by the pool, in the garden, or by the sea, relaxation is guaranteed. The athletically inclined can serve on the hotel's own tennis courts or take part in the range of water sports.
Via San Gallo, Lido 74;
Tel 041/526 15 87.
www.excelsior-venezia.com

Villa Mabapa
A high-class hotel with a lovely view of the lagoon and Venice's old skyline. A privately owned four-star hotel in a 1930s villa, with two further annexes in the beautiful grounds, where guests can also stay. Dinner, served on the magnificent garden terrace in summer, is an unforgettable experience.
Riviera San Nicolo 16, Lido;
Tel 041/526 05 90.
www.villamabapa.com

Nightlife

Club 22
One of Venice's rare clubs, and here the music isn't just recorded, there are regular live gigs. As is typical for this kind of club, the audience turns up quite late in the evening. The DJ normally plays music from the 1970s to the present day.
Lungomare Guglielmo Marconi 22, Lido;
Tel 041/526 04 66;
Fri–Sat 22.00–4.00.

MAJOR MUSEUMS

Venice has a wealth of museums, covering every period of European art from classical times to the present day, Jewish and Oriental culture; there are even those devoted to sea travel and glassware. All of these venerable institutions are overshadowed by the majestic Gallerie dell'Accademia, although the Fondazione Musei Civici and the Museo Correr also have extensive collections. The museum in the Ca' Rezzonico, which is also part of the Fondazione Musei Civici, gives an insight into aristocratic life in the 18th century, and fans of classical modern art should not miss a visit to the Peggy Guggenheim Collection, which offers an overview of all the important movements of classical modernism.

The collection is accommodated in buildings from several periods: the late Gothic abbey church of Santa Maria della Carità, the monastery of the Lateran Canons, built in part by the great Renaissance architect Andrea Palladio, and the Scuola della Carità, built around 1350. The altered classical façade and the entrance were finished by 1756.

INFO

Gallerie dell'Accademia,
Campo della Carità,
Dorsoduro 1050;
Tel 041/ 52 00 345
Mon 8.15–14.00, Tues–Sun
8.15–19.15; Vaporetto:
Accademia. www.gallerie
accademia.org

Vittore Carpaccio: The Legend of St Ursula

This picture cycle was originally kept in the Scuola di Santa Orsola. The artist (c. 1455–1526), a master of the Venetian school, depicts several scenes from the arduous pilgrimage to Rome undertaken by the Breton princess, Ursula, and her retinue of 11,000 maidens, and their subsequent martyrdom in Cologne at

A curious legend: Vittore Carpaccio's *The Arrival of the Pilgrims in Cologne.*

the hands of the Huns and their dreaded king, Attila, during the return journey. The almost anecdotal narrative style, which transposes the action into the world of Venice in about 1500, the detailed, draftsman-like style, and the atmospheric use of light and shade make Carpaccio's greatest work, a saint's life in pictures, a masterpiece. Born in Venice, Carpaccio was a pupil of Bellini. He is renowned for his broad urban scenes showing the power and wealth of the city.

The beginnings of the collection

Venice's artists formed an academy in 1750, following the practice of other cities such as Rome and Paris, where academies had existed for some time. It organized exhibitions and began a collection of works submitted for admission.

Rededication in the Napoleonic period

In 1807, under Napoleonic rule, the academy was transformed into a state art school with a reference collection and housed in the monastery complex of the Carità, after the church and monastery had been stripped of their function and dissolved. The old church decoration was torn out and the interior divided into several rooms. Even the monastery's beautiful Palladian building was changed beyond all recognition.
The collection was augmented enormously with works of art from other churches and monasteries, not to mention individual donations, although the Accademia did not receive much itself, as Napoleon had numerous paintings transported to Milan in Lombardy. Eventually, the gallery was legally separated from the academy.

Early Venetian painting

Venice was long influenced artistically by Byzantium, as

is evidenced by the great mosaic cycles in St Mark's. An inclination toward Western Gothic art does not become visible until around 1350, with Paolo Veneziano (before 1333 to after 1358) and the epoch-making work of Giorgio di Bondone (1266–1337), considered to

Giovanni Bellini's magnificent oil painting, *Sacra Conversazione* (1487–88).

be one of the major predecessors of the Italian Renaissance; it is also visible in the Accademia's *Polyptychon*. From this point on, Venetian art was to develop independently. It was the painting dynasties of the Vivarinis and Bellinis who would dominate the late 15th century.

The heyday of Venice's art

Venice's artistic development reached its first great high point with Giovanni Bellini (c. 1430–1516). The Accademia has several of his

pictures, which were to prove influential on later painting, including the *San Giobbe Altarpiece* and Marian pictures such as *Madonna with Trees*. Even the master Albrecht Dürer (1471–1528) was inspired by Giovanni Bellini during his two trips to Venice.

The same master created the realistic *Portrait of a Young Man* in 1475.

Old masters of the High Renaissance

Giorgione (real name Giorgio Barbarelli da Castelfranco, 1478–1510), Titian (between 1488 and 1490–1576), Paolo Veronese (1528–1588), and Jacopo Tintoretto (1518–1594), who anticipated mannerism, are considered the real masters of the Venetian Renaissance.
The Accademia possesses numerous exceptional works of art, such as Giorgione's *Tempest*, Titian's *Presentation of the Virgin at the*

The Accademia is certainly the city's most important art gallery and offers an overwhelming glimpse of the development of Venetian painting from its beginnings to the 18th century. The collection is distinguished by world famous individual paintings and complete picture cycles. All the great artists of Venice and the surrounding Veneto are represented – an absolute must for art enthusiasts of every nation (see p. 102).

Temple and the *Pietà*, his last work, Veronese's *Feast in the House of Levi*, and Tintoretto's *Miracle of St Mark*. Venetian painting from this glittering period is characterized by brush strokes creating atmospheric use of light, tonal harmony, and a brilliantly varied palette.

Venetian painting in the 18th century

The second high point of Venetian painting came in the 18th century, when itinerant painters from the lagoon were called to royal and princely courts across the

Tintoretto painted the famed *Miracle of St Mark Freeing the Slave* for the Scuola Grande di San Marco in 1548.

Antonio Canal, known as Canaletto (1697–1768), depicted bustling everyday life in a cheerful baroque setting in his *Capriccio with Ruins and Porta Portello, Padua* (c. 1734).

The great cycles

The Accademia has integrated two great picture cycles from the old confraternity's rooms: *The Miracle of the Relic of the Holy Cross* from the Scuola Grande di San Giovanni Evangelista, in whose creation several artists were involved and which affords an insight into Venetian life and self-perception at the beginning of the 16th century, and Carpaccio's St Ursula cycle, depicting the 4th- or 5th-century princess's pilgrimage to Rome (see box, left).

continent and found that their airy and elegant creations, as well as their depictions of the occasionally dramatic and bizarre, raised the pulses of the collectors and crowned heads of Europe. The Accademia has works by Giovanni Battista Piazzetta (1682–1754) and Giovanni Battista Tiepolo (1696–1770), as well as *vedute* by Canaletto (real name Giovanni Antonio Canal, 1697–1768), Bernardo Bellotto (1722–1780, also called Canaletto), Francesco Guardi (1712–1793), and genre pictures by Pietro Longhi (1702–1785).

A figure of spiritual light in very worldly illumination: Titian's *Presentation of the Virgin at the Temple* (c. 1534–38, detail).

Baldassare Longhena began construction of this palace on the Grand Canal in 1649, but never completed it. In 1751 the Rezzonico family acquired the building and finished the work. In 1936, having become the property of the city of Venice, the palace was turned into a museum, but nonetheless retained all the features of an old family seat.

INFO
*Dorsoduro 3136;
Tel 041/ 241 01 00;
Apr–2 Nov Wed–Mon
10.00–18.00, 3 Nov–
Mar Wed–Mon 10.00–
17.00; Vaporetto: Ca'
Rezzonico.www.musei
civiciveneziani.it*

Pietro Longhi: The Rhinoceros

Pietro Longhi (1702–1785) specialized early in his career on small-scale depictions of scenes from everyday Venetian life, which soon gained great acclaim. His subjects included whimsical conversation pieces set in aristocratic circles and folksy scenes drawn from the city's streets. In his

Longhi's picture, *Rhinoceros*, indirectly critiques Venetian society.

Rhinoceros (1751), he depicted a presentation of this exotic animal, which was shown throughout Europe. But what are the audience doing on their benches? Some are masked or disguised, looking around or at each other, or even out of the picture. Longhi is with gentle irony pointing out that Venetian society in the middle of the 18th century is occupied only with itself and self-representation – Longhi also chronicled the gambling dens that flourished at the time. Some of his work is reminiscent of the English painter Hogarth's.

History of the collection

The paintings and other artistic creations in the museum, even the wall coverings and the frescoes, date only partly from the Rezzonico family's original decoration of the *palazzo*, although this was richly decorated by leading artists after construction was completed. In 1832, a few years after the death of the last member of the Rezzonico

Painted with sensitivity: Lorenzo Tiepolo's *Portrait of Cecilia Guardi-Tiepolo* (1757).

family, the entire portable contents of the house were removed, and the late baroque artworks and delicate rococo furniture you can admire in the museum today form part of Venice's municipal art collection.

More than just donated or purchased furnishings and *objets d'art* are on show here, however: the Magistrate of Venice had wall paintings removed and transported here, such as frescoes by Giovanni Battista Tiepolo (1696–1770) from Palazzo Barbarigo, and others by

Giovanni Domenico Tiepolo (1727–1804) from the Tiepolo family villa in Zianigo, which is now part of Mirano. The latter depict a variety of themes, including allegorical representations and scenes and motifs from mythology and the Commedia dell'Arte.

Second floor

On the *piano nobile*, the main floor of the *palazzo*

A place for celebrations of baroque magnificence: the double-height ballroom (1753–56), painted by Pietro Visconti and Giovanni Battista Crosato.

where social life at Ca' Rezzonico's justly famous parties would have buzzed during the baroque period, there is a large and well-proportioned ballroom, decorated with pomp and style. Frescoes by Giovanni Battista Crosato (1697–1756) look down upon his *Light of the Sun Illuminating the Four Quarters of the Earth* in the centre of the room, and carved furniture by Andrea Brustolon (1662–1732) sets the tone. The ceiling of the Nuptial Allegory room was painted in 1758 to mark the

union of Ludovico Rezzonico and Faustina Savorgnan by no less a personage than Giovanni Battista Tiepolo. His *Phoebus Apollo Brings the Bride in his Triumphal Carriage to the House of Rezzonico* is as impressive as the portrait painted by the famous German artist Anton Raphael Mengs (1728–1779) of Pope Clemens XIII (1693–1769). Clemens was a member of the family known in private life as Carlo della Torre di Rezzonico, elected

pope in 1758. Then there are the rococo decorations in the house chapel, the pastel room with works by Rosalba Carriera (1675–1757) and others, the Gobelin room, the throne room with further frescoes by Tiepolo, and the library. Several rooms are dedicated to Tiepolo and Gregorio Lazzarini (1655–1730), and to furniture and furnishings by Andrea Brustolon. Also known for his sculptures in wood, Brustolon inspired many imitators, working both during and after his time.

Housed in a baroque palace, this collection forms part of Venice's municipal holdings and affords a great insight into the life of the Venetian aristocracy of the 18th century. Magnificent rooms with frescoes, including a masterpiece by G. B. Tiepolo, and paintings by amongst others Canaletto, Guardi, and P. Longhi all combine with precious furniture, chandeliers, silk wallpaper, and porcelain to give an impression of an exuberant era.

Pinacoteca Egidio Martini

Situated on the third floor, this collection was donated to the city at the beginning of the 20th century by the scholar and restorer Egidio Martini. It comprises pictures of equal quality and gives an almost complete overview of the history of Venetian painting, with an emphasis on the 17th and 18th centuries. Every genre is represented

The Ferruccio Mestrovich Collection

The Mestrovich collection, housed in the Browning house, is one of the city's most recent art acquisitions (Ca' Rezzonico was the last home of the poet Robert Browning, who died here on 12 December 1889). A small but extremely valuable collection of 16 objects with religious themes from the 15th to 18th centuries, it was

The Queen of Heaven: Francesco Guardi completed this *Madonna and Child* in 1760 (Mestrovich Collection).

Although known principally for allegorical depictions, the great Tiepolo would occasionally choose more worldly subjects from the aristocratic world, such as this *Greyhound*.

here, from religious *telere* to portraits, from landscapes and *vedute* to seascapes, from depictions of historical scenes to everyday events. Of especial note in this collection of over 300 works are pieces by Cima da Conegliano (*c.* 1460–1517/ 18), Amigoni (1675– 1752), Giovanni Battista Piazzetta (1682–1754), Pietro Longhi (1702–1785), Jacopo Tiepolo, and Rosalba Carriera, who was unusual in being a female Venetian Rococo painter, much admired for her portrait miniatures.

the work of the collector Ferrucio Mestrovich, the scion of a Dalmatian family resident in Venice since 1945. Of particular note are works by Cima da Conegliano, Jacopo Tintoretto (1518–1594; *Portrait of Francesco Gherardini*), and Jacopo Amigoni (*Portrait of a Lady* and *Portrait of a Young Woman*). There are also works by old masters such as Francesco Guardi (1712–1793) and Alessandro Longhi (1730– 1833; *Portrait of Giuseppe Cherubini*), which really make the visit worthwhile.

A man become God: Benedetto Diana's *Christ Benedictory* (completed after 1480, Mestrovich Collection).

Construction of the shorter wing of the Procuratie lining St Mark's Square was begun in 1810 under French rule, and for this reason it is known as the Napoleonic Wing (Ala Napoleonica). It was used as function rooms for the Procuratie Nuove, at the time and under Habsburg rule a residence, and today houses the exhibition rooms of the museum.

INFO
*Piazza San Marco,
Procuratie Nuove,
Ala Napoleonica; Tel
041/240 52 11; 1 Apr–
2 Nov 9.00–19.00,
3 Nov–31 Mar 9.00–
17.00.www.musei
civiciveneziani.it*

Antonio Canova: Daedalus and Icarus

This group of mythological sculptures in the throne room is considered the most important early work from the Venetian period of the great classical sculptor, Antonio Canova (1757–1822). Daedalus built the labyrinth in ancient Crete, but was kept prisoner there by King Minos. To escape this captivity he fashioned wings out of feathers, stuck together with wax, for himself and his son, Icarus.

Living marble: Canova's *Daedalus and Icarus* group, completed in 1779.

Despite his father's warnings, the son strayed too close to the sun; his wings melted and Icarus fell into the sea and drowned. Daedalus reached Sicily, and in Greece was considered the founding father of art. Canova's figures are realistic and in true classical style regard only one another. Canova was famed for the skill and delicacy with which he rendered naked human flesh in marble.

History of the collection

The scholar Teodoro Correr (1750–1830), after whom the museum is named, bequeathed his extensive collection of documents, objects, and works of art illustrating the history of Venice, and the *palazzo* that contained them, to his home city, with the proviso that a museum be created there. This was opened to the public as early as 1836. Further purchases and donations expanded the holdings to

Antonio Canova, famed throughout Europe in his own lifetime, is considered the greatest sculptor of Italian classicism. Here we see his *Winged Cupid* from 1797.

such an extent that the collection had to be relocated, first to the Fondaco dei Turchi, which now houses the Natural History Museum, with its collections of fossils, flora, and fauna, and aquarium, and then in 1922 to the Procuratie, where it now remains. Since the move, much of the immensely varied collection has been curated thematically and exhibited at various locations throughout the city.

Neo-classical rooms

The museum is entered through the Napoleonic Wing, designed in 1810 by Giuseppe Soli. The magnificent rooms, with their mock antique architectural detailing, frescoes, and decorations in a Pompeiian style, are excellent examples of the formal language of Classicism and the Age of Empire, the predominant style of the Napoleonic period. The staircase, ballroom, throne room, dining room, gallery, drawing room, and all the attendant side rooms were used as official function rooms during the residence of the French and later Habsburg rulers.

The area also houses elegant marble statues and plaster models by Antonio Canova, the most important classical sculptor, who came from the Veneto, including *Daedalus and Icarus* (see box, left). Canova traveled throughout Europe and taught British sculptors John Gibson and Sir Richard Westmacott.

Venetian history and culture

The rooms of the adjoining Procuratie Nuove, originally used for municipal administration, house a section illustrating the history, art, and culture of Venice, with exhibits such as old city plans and maps. The most famous of these exhibits dates from around 1500, the time of Jacopo de'Barbari (*c.* 1440–1515/16).

This part of the collection is mainly concerned with the history of the Venetian doges, however, with numerous portraits and other evidence of the magnificence of those times, such as robes of office and ceremonial garb. Weapons, war supplies, and everything else illustrating Venice's close relationship with the sea is also on display, with images of sea battles and celebrations, coins, documents of everyday life, guilds, and fraternities, and not least of the recreational habits of all classes of the population, achieving a lively reconstruction of many past periods.

Many doges had their portraits painted by famous masters, such as Giovanni Mocenigo, painted by Gentile Bellini in 1478 or 1479, and Pietro Grimani, painted by Pietro Longhi in 1752.

Art and picture collection

The art collection adjoining the historical section is also on the first floor and includes small statues and bronze statuettes, for which

The Museo Correr has over 70 rooms and incorporates the majority of the city's historical and art historical collections and their affiliated picture gallery (*quadreria*). These collections are housed in several different locations, making it the largest museum complex in the world, famous for the number and range of the exhibitions it maintains (see p. 28). The principal building is entered at the west end of Saint Mark's Square opposite the basilica.

Jacopo de'Barbari's *Canal Grande*, a bird's eye view of the city of Venice in about 1500; this detail shows Dorsoduro with the Punta della Dogana, Grand Canal, and San Marco district; a woodcut from a drawing, *c.* 1500.

Venice was particularly well-known from the 15th to the 17th centuries. The picture gallery proper, occupying the second floor, displays works of Venetian art from the beginning of the 16th century and pieces by other artists from all over Italy and the Netherlands.

The evolution of Venetian art was long influenced by Byzantium. An independent Venetian style did not really develop until the 14th century, reaching its first high-point with artists such as Giorgione (1478–1510), Titian (between 1488 and 1490–1576), Veronese (1528–1588), and Tintoretto (1518–1594). Amongst the best-known paintings exhibited in the 19 rooms of the Museo Correr's upper floor are *The Dead Christ* by Antonello da Messina (*c.* 1430–1479), *Pietà* by Giovanni Bellini (*c.* 1430–1516), *The Two Courtesans* by Vittore Carpaccio (*c.* 1455–1526), and a *Madonna* by Lorenzo Lotto (1480–1557). Even the Cretan, El Greco (1541–1614), is represented with two works,

a *Last Supper* and *St Augustine at Prayer*.

Having developed its own style, an intense artistic rivalry soon developed between Venice and Rome and Florence. The debate centered around the use of color versus draftsmanship. Venetians, such as Titian, championed color. Living in a city that was a gateway for the hinterland of Europe, Venetian artists could exploit the materials and pigments that entered the city during trade. They were also quick to adopt oils, which were better able to withstand the humid atmosphere of Venice in which frescoes and tempera soon deteriorated. The beautiful light of the city also played its part.

Gabinetto Stampe e Disegni del Museo Correr

The museum also houses a library and print collection whose holdings are exhibited to the public in rotation.

Antonello da Messina (*c.* 1430–1479): *Pietà* (*The Body of Christ, Supported by Three Angels*; *c.* 1476, oil on wood).

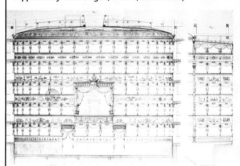

The Teatro La Fenice has had an eventful history; completed in 1791, it burned down in 1836, was rebuilt, and then went up in flames again in 1996. The lavish refurbishment was completed in 2004. Lithograph by Giovanni Battista Meduna, 1836 or 1837.

Construction of the Palazzo Venier dei Leoni on the Grand Canal was begun for the Venier family in 1749 by Lorenzo Boschetti, but never completed. Not until the beginning of the 20th century was enough work completed to at least make it habitable. In 1949 the building was purchased by Peggy Guggnhiem, who lived there amongst her collection of *objets d'art* until her death.

INFO
Palazzo Venier dei Leoni, Dorsoduro 704; Tel (041) 240 54 11; Wed–Mon 10.00–18.00; Vaporetto: Accademia or Salute Da Piazza San Marco. www. guggenheim-venice.it

The Italian futurists

This group of fine artists, writers, musicians, and architects was formed in Italy in 1909 and published its opinions on modern art and culture. There was unqualified approval for modern technology, the speed of modern progress, and the dynamics in life that resulted from industrialization. The futurists rejected anything connected with tradition,

Umberto Boccioni, self-portrait (*c.* 1905/06).

encouraging the progress of modernism across Europe. Along with this went a glorification of war and an image of humanity with a strengthened will that excluded romanticism, love, pain, and feelings of any kind. After World War I, many futurists became fascists, although the greatest artist of the group, Umberto Boccioni, was killed in 1916. Although Italian based, there were futurist movements across Europe and it influenced several later 20th-century art movements, including Surrealism and Dada.

Peggy Guggenheim – Paris, London, and New York

Peggy Guggenheim (1898–1979), a Swiss-German Jewish émigré whose father perished in the *Titanic* disaster of 1912, was a niece of the mine-owner and art-collector Solomon R. Guggenheim (1861–1949), one of America's richest men, although she was not as wealthy.

In 1921, Peggy went to Paris and was introduced by her first husband, Laurence Vail (1891–1968), a Dadaist poet, sculptor, and painter, to many other avant-garde artists, including Marcel Duchamp (1887–1968), Man Ray (1890–1976), and Constantin Brâncusi (1876–1957). Guggenheim sold modern art from a gallery in London between 1938 and 1939, and after her return to New York she established a private gallery to exhibit her collection between 1941 and 1947, which aroused much interest, and to support artists such as Jackson Pollock (1912–1956) and also Max Ernst (1891–1976), to whom she was married between 1942 and 1946.

An American in Venice

Peggy Guggenheim finally returned to Europe in 1947 and settled in Palazzo Venier dei Leoni in Venice in 1949. She was one of modern art's greatest patrons in the 1950s, but also collected African statuary. She did not buy Pop Art, which started to

appear after 1960, or works from the movements that succeeded this, perhaps as she felt no personal connection to these styles. Her grave is in the *palazzo* garden, and in 2003 Yoko Ono planted an olive tree there.

The Peggy Guggenheim Collection

The museum maintains an overview of all the important movements in art that make

Breaking through into modernism: *Mercury Passing in Front of the Sun* by the futurist Giacomo Balla (1914).

up classical modernism. All of the famous names of the period are to be found here, including cubist period works by Pablo Picasso (1881–1973) and Georges Braque

(1882–1963). Early abstract art is represented with a window painting by Robert Delaunay (1885–1941) and a painting by Wassily Kandinsky (1866–1944) from the Blue Rider period. There are also Kandinsky paintings from his Bauhaus period, which effectively illustrate the formal movement toward geometrical abstraction. This transformation was completed when Kandinsky had to return to his Russian homeland as a result of World War I and was exposed to the work of Kasimir Malevitch (1878–1935), who is also represented here.

Italian futurism is represented with paintings and sculptures from artists such

The Peggy Guggenheim Collection is Italy's greatest modern art museum. European abstract and cubist masterpieces are to be found here, along with superb examples of surrealism and abstract impressionism. The museum, which includes the Gianni Mattioli Collection and the Nasher Sculpture Garden, regularly holds superb temporary exhibitions and is part of the Solomon R. Guggenheim Foundation of New York (see p.100). Inaugurated in 1980, the museum is housed in what was Peggy Guggenheim's Venetian home.

as Giacomo Balla (1871–1958), Umberto Boccioni (1882–1916), and Gino Severini (1883–1966), with Giorgio de Chirico (1888–1978) appearing as an example of *pittura metafisica* ("metaphysical painting"). Geometrical reductionist pictures by Piet Mondrian (1872–1944) and works by Theo van Doesburg (1883–1931) indicate their attempts at renewing the Dutch De Stijl group of artists.
Peggy Guggenheim was also an avid collector of the works of surrealist artists. Illustrious names to be found here include Man Ray, Marc Chagall (1887–1985), Joan Miró (1893–1983), René Magritte (1898–1967), Salvador Dalí (1904–1989), and, of course, Max Ernst. The action painting of American abstract impressionism, which succeeded the geometric abstraction of the 1940s, is represented with pieces by Jackson Pollock and Willem de Kooning (1904–1997).

Modern sculpture

The highlights of the sculpture collection include works by Constantin Brâncusi, Henri Laurens (1885–1954), Alberto Giacometti (1901–1966), Henry Moore (1898–1986), Alexander Calder (1898–1976), and *The Angel of the City* by Marino Marini (1901–1980).

The Patsy R and Raymond D Nasher Sculpture Garden

As with the other outdoor sections of the museum, this section displays sculptures

from the main Solomon R. Guggenheim Foundation and works on loan. Artists to be found here include Hans Arp (1886–1966), Max Ernst, Alberto Giacometti, Marino Marini, Andy Goldsworthy (b. 1956), Mario Merz (1925–2003), Henry Moore (1898–1986), and Mimmo Paladino (b. 1948).
Raymond D. Nasher was an American real-estate developer and banker. Along with his wife, Patsy, he assembled one of the world's best collections of Modern and contemporary sculpture with which they filled their Dallas home. Raymond Nasher established a long-term association with the Guggenheim Foundation that enabled him to exhibit some of his pieces at the Peggy Guggenheim Collection here in Venice.

The Gianni Mattioli Collection

This collection of 25 paintings and a drawing is focused on Italian futurism and contains pieces by Umberto Boccioni, Giacomo Balla, Carlo Carrà (1881–1966), and Gino Severini. The composer and painter Luigi Russolo (1885–1947) is also represented.
There is also a portrait of the painter, Frank Haviland, by Amadeo Modigliani (1884–1920) and several still lifes from the early work of Giorgio Morandi (1890–1964). Italian businessman Gianni Mattioli was one of the most important art collectors of the 20th century. He showed great foresight in collecting the work of the Italian-based futurist movement long before it became fashionable.

A futurist icon: Carlo Carrà's *Manifestazione interventista* was created during the war, in 1914.

Diego With Pullover (1953) – sculptures by Alberto Giacometti belong in the heart of classical modernist plastic art.

CITY EXPLORER

CITY WALKS

Many different elements combine to make Venice's magic – the labyrinth of narrow streets and canals, the Piazza San Marco and the giant dome of the cathedral, the Grand Canal, the venerable *palazzi* reflected in the water, the down-to-earth *campi* on Dorsoduro, and the breathtaking view of the campanile belonging to the church of San Giorgio Maggiore. And, of course, the people, with all their vivacity and the elegance of their fashions, traditional carnival masks, exciting *trattorie*, cool bars, bustling markets, and upmarket hotels. If you want to get away from it all, you can take a boat to the islands of the lagoon and discover a world of glassblowers and lacemakers.

Sights

❶ St Mark's Square

What Napoleon called "the finest drawing room in Europe" is the heart of the city. There are pigeons flapping and the sound of Viennese café music, and two giant bronze Moors strike the hours in the clock tower. Surrounding the square, there are the arcades of the Procuratie, the former seat of city government. Nearer the lagoon, the square is bordered by the smaller Piazzetta with its two columns (one topped with the Lion of St Mark, the other with St Theodore) (see p. 24).

❷ St Mark's Basilica

Founded in the early Middle Ages, the church owes its form to Venice's close connections with Constantinople. As was traditional there, the marble-clad cathedral has five domes and is decorated with mosaics, the most beautiful of which are in the right-hand cupola of the entrance hall. Along with the Pala d'Oro, a Byzantine altarpiece in gold, enamel, and precious stones, the domes are some of the cathedral's greatest treasures. Visitors can admire the original antique gilded bronze horses from the façade in the Museo Marciano above the entrance hall, and precious Byzantine gold and silverwork in the treasure room (see p. 34).

❸ Campanile and Loggetta

The view from the tower of St Mark's over the city is almost overwhelming. The edifice, 95 m (312 feet) high and a sym-bol of Venice, collapsed on 14 July 1902, but was immediately rebuilt in its old form. Even Jacopo Sansovino's loggetta at the base of the tower, which suffered some collateral damage, has been rebuilt true to the original. It was originally just a functional building for municipal ceremonies, but the palace guard later moved in here. The wealth of statues hints at Venice's power: the classical deities Minerva, Apollo, and Mercury can be seen, representing science, art, and commerce, as well as a carved stone personification of Peace (see p. 24).

❹ Biblioteca Marciana

Built by Jacopo Sansovino and extending out towards the lagoon, this building is one of the Renaissance highlights of the city. Although undoubtedly the roots of its three-dimensional relief style lie in Rome, where Sansovino was trained, its predilection for intricate decoration and the evenness of form in the long façade are typical of Venice. The Archeological Museum is housed within. The library is now situated near the Zecca, the old mint building (see p. 30).

❺ Doge's Palace

The Venetian Republic's seat of power was originally a fortress surrounded by water, but by the 12th century it was already looking more like a palace than a defensible fortification, with its light and delicate Gothic façade. In the internal courtyard can be found the enormous staircase where the Doge was crowned, and the *palazzo* proper contains the Golden Staircase, function rooms, the great council chambers with their magnificent coffered ceilings, paintings by Titian, Tintoretto, and Paolo Veronese, amongst others, the doge's apartments, and the infamous prisons that lie beyond the Bridge of Sighs (see p. 38).

❻ San Zaccaria

Follow the water down to this church building. Its strong horizontals, rounded gable end, and the classical forms lent to its columns and pillars are all typical of the Renaissance, although the lower portion has a Gothic appearance. *An Enthroned Madonna*, a late work by Giovanni Bellini, can be seen within (see p. 132). It also contains paintings by Antonio Balestra, Van Dyck, Giuseppe Salviati, and Tintoretto, among others.

❼ San Giorgio Maggiore

Back on the quay take a *vaporetto* over to San Giorgio Maggiore. The abbey church here (1566–1610) has rather an entrancing façade, arranging two classical temple frontages together. Two pictures by Tintoretto are especially noteworthy in the interior. The view of Venice from the campanile is spectacular (see p. 110).

❽ Arsenale

The Arsenale, established in 1104, was once a fortified shipyard servicing the universally feared Venetian navy; by 1420, 16,000 shipwrights were employed here. Nowadays, the only things made here are the universally adored Venetian ship's biscuits (see p. 140).

Shopping

❶ Venetia Studium

Mariano Fortuny, an Italian fashion designer, painter, sculptor, architect, and interior designer, has created designs for the hand-painted silk lampshades here as well as numerous other high-quality furnishings. There are beautiful silk evening bags to be found in a variety of shades and a wide selection of fine fabrics. The result is a

From left: St Mark's Square in the morning, warm sunlight flooding through the arcade of the Doge's Palace; the stately interior of the Caffé Quadri; external views of the Al Covo restaurant.

FROM ST MARK'S SQUARE TO THE ARSENALE

Venice's political and spiritual hub is also the scene of its greatest concentration of public life, with many cafés and elegant stores. A stroll around the old shipyard is only a boat trip away on the island of San Giorgio Maggiore.

real shopping experience for the senses!
Calle Larga XXII Marzo;
Tel 041/522 92 81.
www.venetiastudium.com

2 Bottega Veneta
Elegant and beautifully worked leather goods, especially handbags, and a great selection of modern, sometimes extravagant shoes are to be found here – everything is smart, but quite expensive as well.

Calle Vallaresso;
Tel 041/522 84 89.

3 Jesurum
Real Venetian lace is still made on Burano, and this can be admired at Jesurum, as can the historical feel of the shop. Anyone not daunted by the high prices will find elegant table linen, lace, and lots of attractive pieces of embroidery. There is also an outlet shop at Via Bellotto 30, Mestre.

Via Bellott 30;
Tel 041/71 33 00.
www.jesurum.it

4 Martinuzzi
This exclusive store stocks beautifully finished lace items made by hand to old patterns and designs. The quality is very high, as are the prices.
Piazza San Marco 56–59;
Tel 041/520 56 41;
closed Wed (winter).
www.caffeflorian.com

Eating and drinking

1 Caffè Florian
Florian has always been one of Venice's top cafés, and stucco, mirrors, and wall paintings lend the interior its typical coffee-house atmosphere. All this comes at a price, and you'll find an extra charge for the orchestra on your bill. An espresso at the bar is a lot more reasonable.
Piazza San Marco 56–59;
Tel 041/520 56 41;
closed Wed (winter).
www.caffeflorian.com

2 Caffè Quadri
There is another coffee house opposite Florian, in no way inferior to its competitor as far as quality and prices are concerned, and with a tempting restaurant on the first floor with the best view.
Piazza San Marco 120;
Tel 041/528 92 99;
closed Mon (winter).
www.quadrivenice.com

3 Al Covo
Innovative cooking based on Venetian recipes, dished up in a side street behind the strolling ground of the Riva degli Schiavoni. The Benelli family have been serving fish since 1987, often with delightfully fresh vegetables from their own garden.
Castella 3968;
Tel 041/522 38 12;
closed Wed and Thurs.
www.ristorantealcovo.com

4 Trattoria Sottoprova
This *trattoria* is situated away from the hordes of tourists, and even the locals come in to try the pizza.
Via Garibaldi;
Tel 041/520 64 93;
closed Mon.

Isola di San Giorgio Maggiore

Sights

❶ Santa Maria Gloriosa dei Frari

A late Gothic building that was once the abbey church of the Franciscan monastery. The large preaching area and the bare form are typical of mendicant orders such as the Franciscans. A contrast to this is formed by the church's rich ornamentation, donated by the families whose burial vaults are here. The Frari church's best-known works of art include *The Assumption of the Virgin* by Titian (who is also buried here), which hangs in the choir, and his *Pesaro Madonna* in the left transept. There is also Giovanni Bellini's *Madonna and Child with Saints* in the sacristy and Donatello's *St John the Baptist* (see p. 84).

❷ Scuola Grande di San Rocco

The Venetian *scuole* were the headquarters of various fraternities, which were either national or religious groups, and consisted of a chapel, a hospital, and various communal rooms. The members took care of the sick, the old, and the recently deceased. The Scuola Grande di San Rocco is the only one still to retain its complete original decoration. Between 1564 and 1588 Tintoretto painted striking scenes from the life of the Virgin for the ground floor, scenes from the life of Jesus on the walls of the Upper Hall on the top floor, and scenes from the Old Testament on its ceiling. The hotel's hall has a ceiling depicting St Roch and wall frescoes depicting the Passion of Christ (see p. 90).

❸ San Rocco

This church, dedicated to the protector against plague, St Roch, is largely 18th-century but possesses works by Tintoretto dating back to the *scuola*. These depict scenes from the lives of St Roch and Jesus, and afford an insight into the master painter's early work. Continue across one of Venice's most down-to-earth and lively squares, Campo Santa Margherita.

❹ Scuola Grande dei Carmini

Situated next to the Carmelite church (with two works by Cima da Conegliano and Lorenzo Lotto), this *scuola* has a cycle of pictures by Tiepolo. The painting *The Virgin of Carmel Giving the Scapula to St Simeon Stock* (the scapula being the garb of the Carmelite order) is surrounded by depictions of the virtues and miracles associated with Simeon Stock. In contrast to Tintoretto's portentous imagery, Tiepolo's painting style is airy and light, with a sophisticated palette.

❺ San Sebastiano

This simple Renaissance church conceals a particular treasure. Between 1553 and 1556, Paolo Veronese painted the ceilings of the nave and the sacristy (access beneath the organ). Such ceiling paintings only became fashionable in Venice quite late, and San Sebastiano is the oldest example, often serving as a model for later designs. In the sacristy, Veronese has painted the enthroned Virgin and the four Evangelists, and in the church itself there are scenes from the Old Testament story of Esther. Some of the wall paintings are also by Veronese, as is the altarpiece and the organ loft. The master painter was buried beneath the organ in 1588.

❻ Gesuati

The 18th-century church of Santa Maria del Rosario takes its nickname from the Gesuati order, who used to be based here but were replaced by the Dominicans before the church was built. Ceiling frescoes by Giovanni Battista Tiepolo, illustrating the life of St Dominic, are to be found in the interior, and amongst the altar pictures there are examples of work by the masters Sebastiano Ricci, Tintoretto, Piazzetta, and, once again, Tiepolo.

❼ Il Redentore

The Church of the Redeemer, a late work by Andrea Palladio, was commissioned in 1576, at the height of a plague epidemic in Venice, and completed in 1592. In thanks for deliverance from the plague, the doge and his retinue undertook an annual procession from St Mark's across a pontoon bridge to the church, and the feast of the Redeemer is still celebrated on the third Sunday in July. The church façade has Palladio's characteristic layered gable motif and the interior is dominated by a brilliant white. Inside the church are works by Leandro Bassano, Francesco Bassano, Lazzaro Bastiani, Paolo Veronese, Carlo Saraceni, Francesco Bissolo, and Rocco Marconi, among others. Once back on the Dorsoduro, the Accademia is a stone's throw away.

Shopping

❶ C'era una Volta

The name of this toy shop is also its motto: "once upon a time...", and their stock in trade includes beautiful toys of a nostalgic bent, including lots of dolls, of course, as well as teddy bears and stuffed animals in all sizes, and some nice kitsch and bits and pieces.
Campiello San Pantalon; Tel 041/71 88 99.

❷ Campo Santa Margherita

The market in Campo Santa Margherita near the Rialto Bridge sells fruit, vegetables, flowers, and fresh fish, and is always bustling with shoppers after a bargain.
Mon–Sat 8.00–14.00.

❸ Emporio Pettenello

This shop's stock will raise the pulses of adults and children alike, as it is a real treasure chest of games, dolls, model cars, puppets, and little wooden toys. The magical store has cast its spell over generations of Venetians of all ages.
Campo Santa Margherita; Tel. 041/523 11 67.

❹ Mondonovo Maschere

You can buy Carnival masks just about everywhere in Venice, but Mondonovo makes and sells masterpieces made by artists. Most are in a traditional style, some are modern, but all of them are executed with imagination.
Rio Terà Canal; Tel 041/528 73 44; Mon–Sat 9.00–18.00, closed Sun. www. mondonovomaschere.it

From left: Sculptures, columns, and capitals: the Scuola Grande di San Rocco; Antonio Canova designed his tomb himself; there are Carnival masks like these at Mondonovo Maschere.

FROM SAN POLO TO DORSODURO

Take a stroll through San Polo and Dorsoduro, visiting the great Venetian confraternities and churches, with works by Paolo Veronese and Tiepolo. Palladio's Church of the Redeemer is reached by boat across the Giudecca Canal.

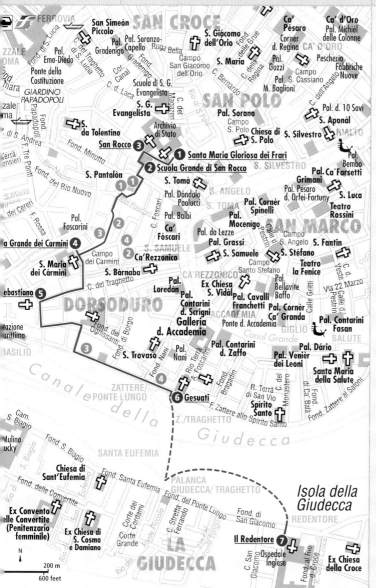

Eating and drinking

① Arca
Pizza is always popular, and the prices are reasonable here. The restaurant is always full and has several other regional dishes and snacks on the menu.
Calle San Pantalon;
Tel 041/524 22 36;
closed Sun.

② Taverna L'incontro
Tourists and students mix with "ordinary" Venetians in this *trattoria*. The proprietor is from Sardinia and has many of his ingredients and wines delivered from the island. Try a meat dish or the spicy rabbit.
Rio Terà Canal;
Tel 041/522 24 04;
closed Mon

③ Ae Oche 2
Pizza and traditional Venetian dishes and snacks can be enjoyed on two floors or even outside beside the canal. If you only want to pop in for a while, have an *ombra*, a chilled glass of wine, and some *cicchetti*, tasty nibbles.
Dorsoduro 1414;
Tel 041/520 66 01;
closing day varies.

④ Gelateria da Nico
If you find yourself strolling along the Zattere, you should make a stop at this ice-cream parlour. On this terrace you can enjoy both the view of La Giudecca and the delicious house specialty: Glandulotto, a confection of frozen nougat immersed in whipped cream – quite heavenly!
Fondamenta Zattere ai Gesuiti;
Tel 041/522 52 93;
closed Thurs.

Sights

❶ Palazzo Labia
Built in 1720 by a merchant family, this *palazzo* situated near the church of St Geremia houses a masterpiece by Giovanni Battista Tiepolo. The Labia family decorated their house lavishly, and Tiepolo provided the frescoes in the ballroom, with scenes from the life of the Egyptian queen, Cleopatra, although the setting has been translated to 16th century Venice (viewings are made by appointment or during concerts).

❷ The Ghetto
In 1516, Venice passed laws forcing Jews to settle in this part of town, and guards were posted at the entrances. The name of the area, derived from the foundries (*geti*) here, soon spread worldwide. The Ghetto was divided into three parts and now has a Jewish museum and a few synagogues that are barely visible from outside, but which can be viewed on a guided tour (see p. 116).

❸ Madonna dell'Orto
This 15th-century abbey church combines Gothic and Renaissance features. Tintoretto's tomb and three of his pictures lie within, and the nearby church of Sant' Alvise has three paintings of the Passion by Giovanni Battista Tiepolo (see p. 120).

❹ I Gesuiti
Built in the early 18th century for the Jesuit order, the church of Santa Maria Assunta dei Gesuiti has a Roman baroque façade designed by Domenico Rossi. The interior contains a famous masterpiece by Titian, *The Martyrdom of St Lawrence* (1558), depicting the saint who was roasted to death, and Tintoretto's *Assumption of the Virgin* (see p. 126).

❺ Santa Maria dei Miracoli
The church was built between 1481 and 1489 by Pietro Lombardo to house a miraculous image of the Virgin. The façade has panels made of different shades of marble, porphyry, and serpentine, and is patterned with quadrilaterals, a false colonnade, and a semicircular pediment. The interior has marble-clad walls with a barrel roof and a cupola over the apse. One of the most beautiful Renaissance buildings (see p. 126).

❻ Santi Giovanni e Paolo
Much like the Frari church, this slightly older Gothic building, known as San Zanipolo, was also used by a mendicant order, this time the Dominicans. It is the largest church in the city and the last resting place of several doges and many noble families, with numerous impressive wall vaults in the interior. There are also notable paintings by masters such as Giovanni Bellini, Lorenzo Lotto, and Paolo Veronese. There are ceiling paintings by Piazzetta in the chapel of St Dominic and a splendid Gothic stained glass window from Murano. One of the earliest modern equestrian statues stands on the square between the church and the decorative Renais-sance façade of the Scuola Grande di San Marco: a masterpiece by Andrea del Verrocchio, the statue of the Venetian mercenary captain, Bartolomeo Colleoni, was made in the late 15th century (see p. 138).

❼ Santa Maria Formosa
This Renaissance church, built by Mauro Codussi, has a baroque tower and a façade from 1604. The interior houses one of the greatest Venetian Renaissance paintings, a picture of St Barbara. The Palazzo Querini-Stampalia museum is nearby (see p. 134). Inside the church are works by Bartolomeo Vivarini, Giambattista Tiepolo, Leandro Bassano, and one of the most celebrated works of Palma the Elder, the St Barbara polyptych.

❽ San Giorgio dei Greci
This 16th-century Greek Orthodox church retained Byzantine traditions into the baroque period. The iconostasis was constructed in the 16th or 17th century in the medieval mosaic tradition.

❾ Scuola di San Giorgio degli Schiavoni
The headquarters of the confraternity of Dalmatians (Slavonians) has a famous picture cycle painted between 1502 and 1507 by Vittore Carpaccio, detailing events from the life of the Dalmatian patron saints George, Trifon, and Hieronymus, from the first's dragon slaying to the last's removal of a thorn from a lion's paw. There are also pictures of the calling of St Matthew and Christ on the Mount of Olives (see p. 132).

Shopping

❶ Libreria Miracoli
A small store, good for browsing, which sells new and second-hand books, especially comics. They have everything about Venice in stock.
Campo Santa Maria Nova; Tel041/523 40 60; 9.00–19.00.

❷ Tipografia Gianni Basso
There is a long history of printing in Venice, but Gianni

From left: The baroque Palazzo Labia; a painting by Palma Il Giovane in Santa Maria dei Miracoli; a statue of St Christopher near the church of Madonna dell'Orto; the Algiubagio bar.

THROUGH CANNAREGIO AND CASTELLO

There is much to admire in Cannaregio: the Ghetto, the tombs of wealthy Venetians in Santi Giovanni e Paolo, great Renaissance painting and charming rococo frescoes, beautiful squares, and several impressive churches.

Basso is one of the few still belonging to this artisan's guild. Good-quality business cards, personal diaries, writing paper, and ex libris sheets are made by hand and sent by mail order all over the world. The printing workshop, although still active, is like a living museum of technology.
Calle del Fumo;
Tel 041/523 4 681;
Mon–Fri 9.00–12.30,
15.00–18.30,
Sat 9.00–12.30.

❸ Rialto market
The Rialto was the city's hub of commerce and trade for centuries. Local farmers and fishermen have been selling their produce here since the Middle Ages. As well as the chefs and restaurateurs, "ordinary" Venetians buy their fruit and vegetables at this central market. The fish market in the Pescheria is held from Tuesday to Saturday between 5.00 and 11.00.
Mon–Sat.

❹ Caffè Costarica
You can enjoy a cup of coffee here surrounded by the scent of freshly roasting beans and secure in the knowledge that fresh reserves can be bought in ground or whole bean form. This coffee roaster's and café has been importing its wares from Costa Rica and Columbia since 1930.
Rio Terà San Leonardo;
Tel 041/71 63 71;
Mon–Sat 8.00–13.00,
15.30–19.30.

Eating and drinking

❶ Al Mascaron
A typical *bacaro*, serving wine and tasty nibbles from morning till night. The menu changes daily and is always fresh and good. Very popular, so booking is recommended. This restaurant has recently celebrated its 30th anniversary. The house specialities are fish-related, but the steak is excellent too.
Calle Lunga Santa Maria Formosa;
Tel 041/522 59 95;
closed Sun.

❷ Enoteca Boldrin
This popular *enoteca* is a good place for reasonably priced, good food. The menu changes daily and unfortunately the wine shop shuts in the early evening.
Salizzada San Canciano;
Tel 041/523 78 59;
from 21.00, daily,
closed Sun.

❸ Fiaschetteria Toscana
A fantastic selection of wines to enjoy with fresh fish and seafood, as well as other typical local dishes such as *fegato alla Veneziana* (calves' liver). A pleasant terrace in the courtyard.
Campo San Giovanni Crisostomo;
Tel 041/528 52 81;
closed Tues.

❹ Algiubagio
A modern bar in a refurbished old building sited right opposite the Fondamente Nuove *vaporetto* stop, this is an ideal stopping-off point for a quick drink or a snack, and there is a nice view from the terrace.
Tel 041/523 60 84.
www.algiubagio.net

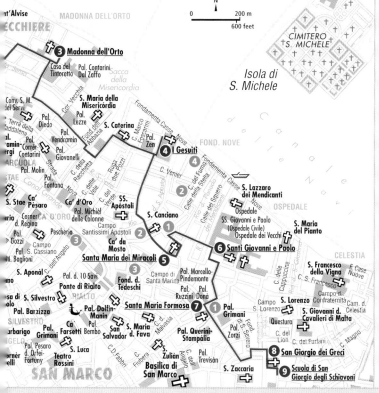

Sights

❶ Grand Canal
Venice's main watery thoroughfare is lined with the city's most splendid palaces and several churches, but crossed by only four bridges: the Ponte Scalze located near the station, the new Calatrava-designed Constitution Bridge, and the Rialto and Accademia Bridges nearer the center. Gondolas and *vaporetti* are the modes of transport of choice on this almost 4-km (2.5-mile) long waterway, which varies between 30 and 70 m (98 and 230 feet) in width and yet on average is only 5 m (16 feet) deep (see p. 56).

❷ Fondaco dei Turchi
Go past the baroque façades of San Simeone Piccolo on the right and the Scalzi church and San Geremia on the left, and opposite the Santa Marcuola *vaporetto* stop you'll find the old warehouse and residence of the Turkish merchants. Its pre-Gothic façade is now sadly only an inexact 19th-century reconstruction, and the building houses the Natural History Museum.

❸ Palazzo Vendramin-Calergi
Diagonally opposite, on the left side of the canal, you will find one of the best examples of early Venetian renaissance architecture, Palazzo Vendramin-Calergi, designed by Mauro Codussi. Its simple proportions and balanced subdivision, with rounded arches, pilasters, and whole-floor lintels, are typical of the period. Richard Wagner died in the Palazzo Vendramin-Calergi on 13 February 1883, and in 1995 the Wagner Museum was opened here, exhibiting manuscript scores, letters, and other mementos. There is also a casino in the *palazzo*.

❹ Ca' Pesaro
If you walk past the baroque façade of San Stae, within which paintings by Tiepolo, Piazzetta, and Sebastiano Ricci are to be found, and Palazzo Mocenigo behind it, you will find the Ca' Pesaro on the right-hand side of the canal. This mighty building by Baldassare Longhena, decorated with heavy columns flanking the windows and many finely sculpted details, is a tutorial in baroque style. The Galleria d'Arte Moderna, displaying works by de Chirico, Boccioni, Bonnard, Chagall, Rouault and Matisse, Klimt, Kandinsky, and Klee, lies within, along with the Museo d'Arte Orientale, whose holdings consist mostly of Japanese works such as lacquerware, weapons, and porcelain from the 17th to the 19th centuries (see p. 68 and p. 72).

❺ Ca' d'Oro
Next on the left is the city's most famous Gothic palazzo, whose façade was once faced with gold, giving the building its name. It was commissioned by the merchant, Marino Contarini, and the head architect was Bartolomeo Bon. The multi-hued, asymmetrical façade features delicate tracery with quatrefoil windows and capitals. Inside the palazzo, the Galleria Franchetti municipal museum is to be found, exhibiting mostly Venetian art from the 14th to the 18th centuries.

❻ Fondaco dei Tedeschi
Completed in 1505 on the same side, just before the Rialto Bridge, this former German merchants' building housed the Venice headquarters of the Italian postal service until 2008. Titian and Giorgione decorated the exterior of the building with now long-lost frescoes (there are fragments in the Galleria Franchetti) and the entire constuction costs were met by the city, so important was trade with the Germans. Wares were delivered here from the Orient and then transported across the Alps. The customs post was right on the canal.

❼ Rialto Bridge
Built between 1588 and 1592 by Antonio da Ponte, Venice's most famous bridge, with its wide, high arch, sweeping steps, splendid views, and souvenir shops was the only way across the Grand Canal until well into the 19th century, and the old commercial base of the city spread out around it. Today's Rialto market is perhaps a small reminder of those days (see p. 64).

❽ Ca' Foscari
The Ca' Foscari, one of Venice's best-known Gothic *palazzi*, is located a bit further along and to the right, and was commissioned by Francesco Foscari, who was doge from 1423 until his death in 1457. The building, with its colonnade, arched windows, and Istrian marble, now belongs to the university. Diagonally opposite, on the other side of the canal, there is the imposing Palazzo Grassi, within which the Pinault Collection is housed. The Ca' Rezzonico, a real Renaissance jewel, is further along on the right side.

❾ Palazzo Corner (Ca' Grande)
Situated only a few houses beyond the Accademia Bridge, construction began on this mighty *palazzo* by

ON THE GRAND CANAL

Enjoy a *vaporetto* trip on the Grand Canal from the Santa Lucia railway station to the Chiesa Santa Maria della Salute, stopping off at famous buildings, museums, and squares. You can walk along the canal by the Rialto Bridge.

Jacopo Sansovino in 1537. A wonderful example of high Renaissance architecture, the building was commissioned by Giacomo Cornaro, a nephew of the king of Cyprus and a scion of one of the city's wealthiest families. Today the *palazzo* is the seat of the Preffetura of Venice. The imposing modern art of the Peggy Guggenheim Collection is based diagonally opposite on the other side of the canal (see p. 100).

⑩ Santa Maria della Salute
Much like Il Redentore, this splendid building is a votive church dedicated after an outbreak of plague. Its location within the cityscape is inspired, and it has become a symbol of Venice. Baldassare Longhena began construction of the baroque church, with its dome and wealth of statuary, in 1631. The reason for its foundation can be seen on the high altar, where an alle-

gorical figure of Venice can be seen kneeling before the Madonna, who is offering her help, chasing away the plague in the form of an old woman. Paintings by Titian, Tintoretto, and Luca Giordano also hang in the church. The Punta della Dogana houses contemporary art (see p. 106). This major new gallery was designed by Japanese architect, Tadao Ando, in the triangular-shaped, old customs house building.

Getting around Venice by boat

Scheduled boats (vaporetti)

Vaporetti, boats run by the municipal transport authority (ACTV) are the most practical and also the cheapest way to get around the city. There are also two night routes. Tickets, which can be bought at the stops, at tourist information offices, at tobacconist's, and on board, should be stamped before the journey, as even unintentional fare-dodging attracts a hefty fine. The timetable varies considerably with the time of year and there are notices at each stop, or a current timetable booklet including fare information for the boat routes and the Lido bus can be obtained from the ACTV. Prices are different for tourists and locals, and there is a choice of single tickets or 24, 48, and 72-hour passes. *ACTV (Azienda del Consorzio Trasporti Veneziani), Piazzale Roma; Tel 01 12 72 21 11. www.actv.it*

Venice Connected

It might be worth pre-paying for some services through Venice Connected, qualifying you for various price reductions on services. As well as transport, Venice Connected enables you to pre-pay for other services such as car parking and even toilets, along with entrance to museums. You are issued with a unique PNR number. Prices will be higher if you pay on the spot once in the city. For more details, see the website and buy your PNR ahead of your trip. *www.veniceconnected.com*

Sights

❶ San Michele
The trip to Murano takes you past the high walls and cypress trees of this Venetian cemetery island. Citizens have been buried here since the 19th century; before then there were graveyards in the city itself, or tombs in the churches. The cemetery church was built by Mauro Codussi. Several famous people have been buried here, including the composers Ermanno Wolf-Ferrari, Igor Stravinsky, and Luigi Nono, the dancer Sergei Diaghilev, the writers Ezra Pound and Joseph Brodsky, and the Argentinian football coach, Helenio Herrera (see p. 148).

❷ Murano
Like Venice itself, Murano is composed of several islands

and its famous glass workshops have been located here since 1291, when the Venetians moved their furnaces out of the town because they were a fire hazard. Elegantly patterned, thin-sided, transparent luxury glassware made the Venetian glass trade one of Europe's finest and its trade secrets were guarded as jealously as state secrets; glassblowers were not even allowed to emigrate. Eventually a few did manage to leave and started producing Venetian-style glass elsewhere, but crystal glass, mostly produced in Bohemia, did not succeed in replacing the fine, locally manufactured products until the 19th century. The manufacture of mirrors and chandeliers continued to flourish, however, and the modern glass industry is once again

an important branch of commerce. Many of the workshops allow visitors to come inside and watch the glass being blown and worked (see p. 148).

❸ Museo del Vetro
The Glass Museum in the old bishop's palace exhibits valuable and often beautiful glassware from classical to modern times. The oldest Murano glassware is from the 15th century, including Angelo Barovier's 1475 enamelled wedding cup. The development of glassmaking techniques such as enamelling, frosting, engraving, and *millefiori* is illustrated, and mirrors and chandeliers demonstrate the skill of Venetian artisans.

❹ Santi Maria e Donato
Once the diocesan cathedral of the bishop of Torcello and Murano, this impressive Romanesque building was begun in the 12th century. The pillared arches on the exterior of the choir are particularly beautiful. There are magnificent floor mosaics inlaid with glass and the apse has retained a really splendid 12th-century Byzantine mosaic of the Madonna.

❺ San Pietro Martire
Work on this former Dominican abbey church was begun in 1474, after its predecessor had been destroyed by fire, and it houses a masterpiece by Giovanni Bellini, the *Barbarigo Altarpiece*, which has retained its original frame. It is complemented with two paintings by Paolo Veronese and also by an *Assumption of the Virgin* from Bellini's workshop.

❻ Burano
The island of Burano, with its brightly painted fishermen's cottages, is famous for lacemaking. In the 16th and 17th centuries, Venetian lace was renowned as the finest in the world, but trade went rapidly downhill in the next hundred years, only recovering in the 19th century after much careful promotion. Real Burano lace costs the earth and very little is now made in the traditional manner since it is such a painstaking process that it pushes prices sky high (see p. 152).

❼ Museo del Merletto
The Lace Museum and the adjoining lacemaking school have been open since 1981, exhibiting valuable Venetian lace, patterns, and objects illustrating the laborious manufacturing process.

❽ San Martino
This church, with its striking leaning tower, has an early baroque *Crucifixion* by Giovanni Battista Tiepolo.

❾ Torcello
Torcello is said to be the oldest continuously populated part of Venice. The island is almost uninhabited now, but was once an important see and is older than Venice. Founded in 639 by the citizens of Altinum, who had fled from the Langobards, this once mighty commercial town was overtaken by its competitor, Venice, in the 15th century and subsequently declined. The two large churches with their art treasures and the two palaces bear witness to Torcello's former greatness (see p. 154), but many of its buildings

From left: An atmospheric evening in a Burano street; a shimmering Byzantine apse mosaic in Santa Maria Assunta on Torcello; a little flower stall on Murano.

FROM SAN MICHELE TO TORCELLO

The boat trip to the lagoon islands should not be missed – there are pretty houses, old churches, and charming scenery, not to mention glass workshops on Murano and lacemaking on Burano, all making for a varied excursion.

were plundered for building material by the departing inhabitants. More recently, Ernest Hemingway spent some time here, and met the woman on whom he based one of the characters in his novel *Across the River and Into the Trees*, which is set in Venice. The island is also featured in British writer Harold Pinter's play *Betrayal*.

⑩ Santa Maria Assunta
The church was founded by the emperor Heraclius around 640, but its modern appearance dates back to about 1000. The interior retains wonderful 11th-century floor patterning and capitals, parts of an even older chancel, and a Byzantine iconostasis with marble reliefs. Almost supernatural mosaics of the Madonna in the apse and of the Last Judgment on the

entrance wall date from the same period.

⑪ Santa Fosca
The main building dates from the 11th century, although the outlying portions are not so old. The interior is dedicated to St Fosca, an early Christian martyr from Ravenna.

⑫ Archeological Museum
Exhibits from prehistoric and classical times as well as church treasures from Torcello's heyday are to be found here. Of particular note is the fine Pala d'Argento from the cathedral, an altarpiece much like the Pala d'Oro in St Mark's. An ancient stone seat is claimed to have been the throne of the once dreaded Attila, king of the Huns and the "scourge of God".

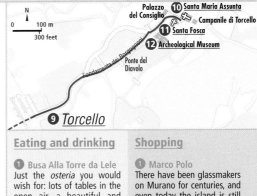

⑨ *Torcello*

Eating and drinking

① Busa Alla Torre da Lele
Just the *osteria* you would wish for: lots of tables in the open air, a beautiful and atmospheric square enjoying Mediterranean sunshine late into the evening, and portions of food that lack nothing as far as taste and quality are concerned. There are excellent fish and seafood dishes, and the desserts, such as the homemade *tiramisù*, are to die for.
Campo Santo Stefano 3, Murano;
Tel 041/73 96 62;
closed Mon evenings.

② Da Romana
The fame of this *trattoria* on the island of Burano has spread far beyond the city, and Venetians will happily take the short boat trip to taste such delicious fare. Fish dishes, traditionally grilled over a charcoal fire, are a strong point. Run by the Barbaro family, Da Romano is a popular meeting place for artists – consequently the walls are covered with all manner of artwork. Note the opening times.
Piazza Galuppi 221, Burano;
Tel 041/73 00 30;
closed Sun evenings and Tues in summer, closed all winter.

Shopping

① Marco Polo
There have been glassmakers on Murano for centuries, and even today the island is still full of glassmaking factories, showrooms, and gift shops. Not all the pieces are terribly tasteful, but you should be able to find something you like. You can watch the glassblowers sweat over their laborious work here, and then choose from a great selection of glassware in the gift shop. There is also an interesting exhibition of typical glass products, which is worth a look. There are also, of course, modern and contemporary designs wrought from this fragile raw material.
Fondamenta Manin 1, Murano;
Tel 041/73 99 04.
www.marcopologlass.it

② Merletti dalla Olga
The tiny island of Burano with its brightly painted houses is the place to go for excellent *merletti* (lace), and there is a good range at Olga's. It is worth getting expert advice, as much of what is for sale in the area is just cheap imported lace.
Piazza Galuppi 105, Burano;
Tel 041/73 02 83.
www.olgalace.com

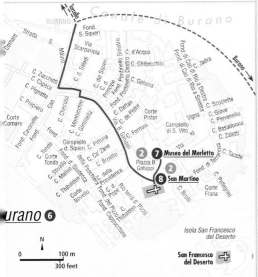

Venice has more than 400 bridges: the Ponte della Libertà connects the city with the mainland; four larger bridges span the Grand Canal, and there are many other smaller ones, such as the Ponte del Megio in Santa Croce.

KEY

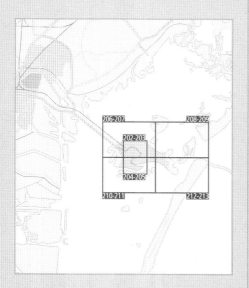

═══════════	Motorway (freeway)
───────────	Primary route (arterial road)
───────────	Other road
───────────	Side (local) road
───────────	Footpath
─━─━─━─━─	Railway (railroad)
─┼─┼─┼─┼─	Industrial railway (railroad)
· · · · · · · · ·	Passenger ferry
───────────	Ferry
🛳	Ferry terminal
🚢	Car ferry

CITY ATLAS

The maps in the City Atlas section give detailed practical information to help make your stay more enjoyable. Clear symbols indicate the position of buildings and monuments of note, facilities and services, public buildings, the transport network, and built-up areas and green spaces (see the key to maps below).

	Densely built-up area; Thinly built-up area
	Public building
	Building of note; Industrial building
	Green space; Wooded area
+++ LLL	Cemetery; Jewish cemetery
	Mudflats
⟱	Principal train station
ES IC/EC	Express train station
🚄	Regional and main line train station
🚌	Bus station

11	Major road number	⟱	Water taxi
✈	Airport	🦢	Gondola landing stage
🏟	Stadium	✝	Church
⛺	Youth hostel	✡	Synagogue
P P	Car park; Multi-story car park	☪	Mosque
🌴	Beach	🗼	Tower
Grand Hotel	Hotel	🎭	Theater
ℹ	Information	M	Museum
✉	Post office	📖	Library
✚	Hospital	💡	Lighthouse
𝕀	Column/monument	Güter	Freight depot

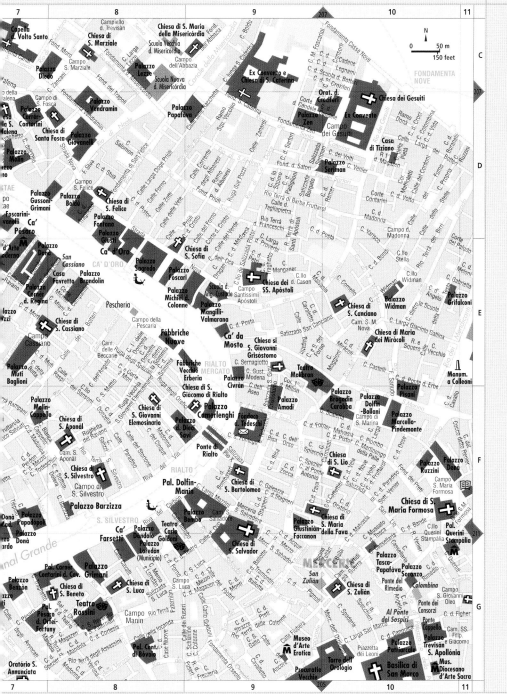

N

0   200 m
600 feet

Ponte della Libertà

11

Ponte della Libertà

Ponte della
Ferrovia

*Isola San
Secondo*

Canale s secondo

Laguna secondo

Canale-dell

SACCA DI
ALOISE
Fond. Cor

SACCA DI
SAN GIROLAMO
Fond. delle Cappu

Fond. delle Capu
Fond. Giustinian
C. d.
cooperativa
Fond. di S. Giobbe
Rio del Battell
Fond. di S. Girolamo
Cpl. delle Beccarie
C. delle Beccarie
Pal. Surian
Le
Cappu
C. della Ceraria
C. S. Giobbe
Fond.
S. Giobbe
C. d. due
Corti
P
Nar
Rio di Cannaregio
Hesperia
Rialto sav
PARCO
SAVORG
Pal. Zeno
S. Ger

*Nuova Isola del
Tronchetto*

Canale Colombola

Rio della Cret

Canale-della

P

P

P

P

TRONCHETTO B

Mercato
Ittico

Capitaneria
di Porto

Ponte della
Libertà

C. Priuli
dei Cappu

ES
IC/EC

Güter

Chiesa
degli Stalzi

San Simec
Piccolo

Ex Convento
di S. Chiara

Stazione
S. Lucia

Pal. Pal
Gradenigo Sor

Palafenice

Canal Grande

Fond. di S. Lucia

Lista di Spagna

Lista di Spagna

FERR

Pal. C

Pal.
della Lana

PIAZZALE
ROMA

Stazione
Marittima Merci

Chiesa di
S. Nome
di Gesù

Autorimessa

Pal.
Emo-Diedo

Cor. di S. Andrea

Liberta

Fond. di S. Chiara

GIARDINO
PAPADOPOLI

Pal.
della Lana

Evange

TRONCHETTO

Ex Chiesa di
S. Andrea

Campo
d.Lana

Fond.
Papadopoli

Pullman Park

Piazzale
Roma

C. della
Chiovere

S.
da Tolentino

Bacino Stazione
Marittima

Canale Scomenzera

R. Terra di
S. Andrea

Fond. di S. Andrea

Fond. della
Fabbrica dei Tabacchi

Fond. Minotto

S. R

210

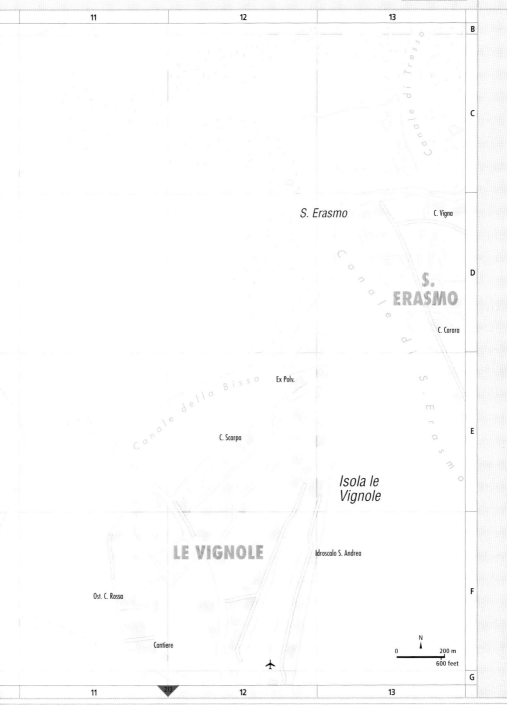

B

Canale di Tresso

C

S. Erasmo

C. Vigna

D

S.
ERASMO

Canale di S. Erasmo

C. Carara

Canale della Bissa

Ex Polv.

E

C. Scarpa

Isola le
Vignole

LE VIGNOLE

Idroscalo S. Andrea

F

Ost. C. Rossa

Cantiere

N

0   200 m
         600 feet

G

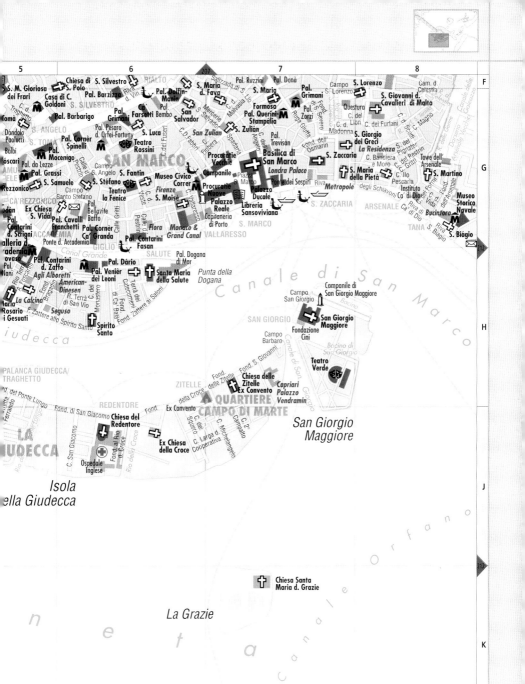

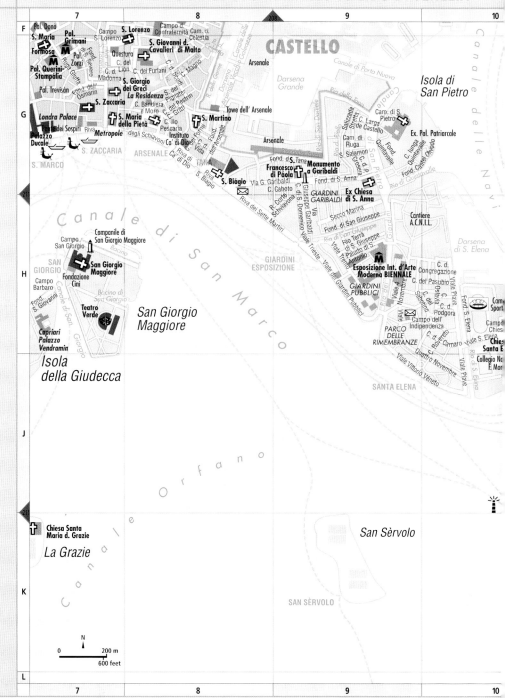

CASTELLO

Isola di
San Pietro

Pol. Donà
S. Maria
Formosa
Pal. Grimani
Pal. Zorzi
C. del Lion
Pal. Querini-Stampália
Pal. Trevisán
Campo S. Lorenzo
S. Lorenzo
Campo d. Confraternità
Cam. d. Celestia
S. Giovanni d. Cavalieri di Malta
Questura
C. dei Furlani
S. Giorgio dei Greci
La Residenza
Londra Palace
Ponte dei Sospiri
S. Zaccaria
S. Maria della Pietà
Metropole
S. ZACCARIA
Palazzo Ducale
S. MARCO
ARSENALE

Arsenale
Darsena Grande
Towe dell' Arsenale
S. Martino
Arsenale
Instituto Ca' di Dio
Riva Ca' di Dio
Riva degli Schiavoni
Francesco di Páola
S. Biágio
Monumento a Garibaldi
Via G. Garibaldi
Giardini Garibaldi
Ex Chiesa di S. Anna
Riva dei Sette Martiri

Cam. di S. Pietro
Ex Pal. Patriarcale
Cam. di Ruga
Cantiere A.C.N.I.L.

Campanile di San Giorgio Maggiore
Campo San Giorgio
San Giorgio Maggiore
Fondazione Cini
Campo Barbaro
Teatro Verde
Capriari Palazzo Vendramin

SAN GIORGIO
Bacino di San Giorgio

San Giorgio Maggiore

Isola della Giudecca

Canale di San Marco

GIARDINI ESPOSIZIONE

Secco Marina
Fond. di San Giuseppe
Esposizione Int. d'Arte Moderna BIENNALE
GIARDINI PUBBLICI
PARCO DELLE RIMEMBRANZE
SANTA ELENA

Darsena di S. Elena

Cam Sport
Campo Chies
Chies Santa E
Collegio N F. Mor

Canale delle Navi

Canale Orfano

Chiesa Santa Maria d. Grazie
La Grazie

San Sèrvolo

SAN SÈRVOLO

N
0   200 m
600 feet

F

✈

Porto di Lido

G

Isola la Certosa

Canale San Nicolò

Riviera S. Nicolò

Via del Diávolo

Via dei San Micheli

Piazzale S. Nicolò

✝ **S. Nicolò**

H

Aeroporto G. Nicelli (Aereo Club G. Ancillotto)

✈

S. NICOLÒ

Via Morandi

Riviera San Nicolò

Campo Sportivo

Via G.

ola di anta Elena

ANTICO CIMITERO ISRAELITICO

Selva

L L

S. NICOLÒ

✝ CIMITERO CATTOLICO

Tiro a Segno

J

PIAZZALE R. RAVA

Via Cipro

Villa Mabapa

Via Morea

CIMITERO ISRAELITICO

Lido di Venézia

Riviera San Nicolò

Via Marco Polo

Via A. Manuzio

Via Cipro

Via P. Manuzio

Strada dietro Tosorio Marino

Ospedale al Mare e Pronto Soccorso

SPIAGGIA COMUNALE

Via Francesco Duodo

Via Soszer Tiro

Via Foscarini

Via Rovigno

Via Fra' Mauro

Via Caboto

D'Annunzio

Via Cipro

Via Perento

SPIAGGIA OSPEDALE AL MARE

Via Aquileia

Via Orseolo

Via Nicossa

Via Cipro

Via Cipro

Via Caboto

Piazza Pola

S. MARIA ISABETTA

Témpio Votivo

Riviera S. Maria Elisabetta

Via P. Smirne

Via Bardari

Via Fra' Paolo

S. Maria Elisabetta

Via Corfù

Via Perasto

Via Negroponte

Via A. Loredan

Piazza Pola

K

Piazzale S. Maria Elisabetta

Via Paolo Erizzo

Via Zara

Via C. Zeno

Lungomare Gabriele

Via Sandro Gallo

Via Doge Dom.

Via Lepanto

Via Scutari

Via Cipro

Via Famagosta

Via V. Pisani

Michièl

Via Spalato

Via Enrico

Pubblica Sicurezza

Dándolo

Piazzale Bucintoro

Gran Viale S. Maria Elisabetta

Terazza a Mare

ZONA COMUNALE

L

Litorale di Lido

CITY ATLAS: STREET INDEX

INDEX OF KEY PEOPLE AND PLACES

IMPORTANT ADDRESSES AND WEBSITES

International Code for Italy:
00 39

Emergency:
Tel 112 (police, ambulance, fire, also for mobiles)

Ambulance:
Ospedale Civile
Tel 04 15 29 41 11

Venice on the internet:
www.comune.venezia.it
www.turismovenezia.it
www.veniceinfo.it

Enit – Ente Nazionale Italiana per il Turismo
(Italian State Tourist Board)
In the UK:
1, Princes Street
London W1B 2AY
Tel 00 44/20 74 08 12 54
Fax 00 44/20 73 99 35 67
italy@italiantouristboard.co.uk

In the United States:
630, Fifth Avenue, Suite 1565
New York NY 10111
Tel 001/212 245 56 18
Fax 001/212 586 92 49
enitny@italiantourism.com

12400, Wilshire BLVD, Suite 550
Los Angeles CA 90025
Tel 001/310 820 18 98
Fax 001/310 820 63 57
enitla@italiantourism.com

500, North Michigan Avenue 2240
Chicago IL 60611
Tel 001/312 644 09 96
Fax 001/312 644 30 19
enitch@italiantourism.com

In Canada:
175 Bloor Street E., Suite 907 South Tower
Toronto M4W 3R8
Tel 001/416 925 48 82
Fax 001/416 925 47 99
enitto@italiantourism.com

In Australia:
PO Box Q802, QVB NSW 1230
Level 4, 46 Market Street Sydney
NSW 2000
Tel 00 61/02 92 62 16 66
Fax 00 61/02 92 62 16 77
italia@italiantourism.com.au

Lost Property:
Municipio di Venezia
Palazzo Farsetti-Loredan
Tel 04 12 74 82 25

Rail Information:
Tel 04 178 52 38

Bus station:
Tel 04 12 72 28 38

Airport:
Tel 04 12 72 21 79

British Consulate Venice
Piazzale Donatori di Sangue 2
(also known as 'Piazzale Sicilia')
30171 Venezia – Mestre
Tel 00 39/041 505 59 90
Fax 00 39/041 95 02 54
britconvenice@tin.it

Embassy of United States in Rome
Palazzo Margherita
Via Vittorio Veneto, 119/a
00187 Roma
Italy
Tel 00 39/06 467 41
Fax 00 39/06 488 26 72 or 00 39/06 46 74 22 17
http://rome.usembassy.gov

Embassy of Canada in Rome
Via Zara 30
Rome, Italy
00198
Tel 00 39/06 854 44 29 11
00 39/06 85 44 41
Fax 00 39/06 854 44 29 12
http://www.ltaly.gc.ca
rome.citizenservices@international.gc.ca

Australian Embassy in Rome
Via Antonio Bosio, 5
Rome 00161
Italy
Tel 00 39/06 85 27 21
Fax 00 39/06 85 27 23 00
http://www.italy.embassy.gov.au/
info-rome@dfat.gov.au

Picture credits

Abbreviations:
M = Mauritius
t. = top
b. = bottom
l.= left,
r.= right
m. = middle

Front cover: large image: Lubenow/LOOK; image l.: Pflegar/Panthermedia; image m.: akg/Cameraphoto; image b.: Schaefer/ Panthermedia. Cover back l.: Look/Sabine Lubenow; m.: Corbis/Marco Christofor; b.: laif/ Hemis.

p. 1 and 2/3: H. + D. Zielske; p. 4/5: laif/hub; p. 6/7: Huber/G. Simeone; p. 8/9: Corbis/The Gallery Collection; p. 10 t. and l.: akg/Cameraphoto; p. 10 m.: M/ imagebroker/Lubenow; p. 10 m.: Huber/Guido Baviera; p. 11 l.: Corbis/Alinari Archives; p. 11 r.: Huber/Johanna Huber; p. 12 t.: akg/Cameraphoto; p. 12 l.: akg/North Wind Picture Archives; p. 12: Bridgemanart; p. 13 t. and m.: akg/Cameraphoto; p. 13 t.r.: Huber/Johanna Huber; p. 13 b. r.: akg/Cameraphoto; p. 13 m.: Huber/ Johanna Huber; p. 14 t. 1: akg/Erich Lessing; p. 14 t. 2: Bridgemanart/Alinari; p. 14 t. 3: Bridgemanart; p. 14 t. 4: akg/Electa; p. 14 l. and m. b.: akg/Cameraphoto; p. 14/15 m.: akg; p. 15 t. 1 and 2: akg/Cameraphoto; p. 15 t. 3 and 4: akg/Erich Lessing; p. 15 r. m.: akg/Cameraphoto; p. 15 b. r.: laif/Gurian; p. 16 t.: Bridgemanart; p. 16 l.: laif/VU; p. 16 r. (three) and 17 t. (two): akg/Cameraphoto; p. 17 t. r.: F1 online/ p. Tauqueur; p. 17 b. r.: Corbis/Marco Christofori; p. 18 t. l. and r.: akg/ Bianconero; p. 18 l.: Visum/SINTESI; p. 18 m.: akg/Cameraphoto; p. 19 t. l.: peitschphott.com/Peter Peitsch; p. 19 t. r.: Corbis/Micheline Pelletiere; p. 19 l.: Artur/Christian Richters; p. 19 t. r.: laif/ Hemis; p. 19 b. l. and b. r.: Huber/Guido Baviera; p. 20/21: H. + D. Zielske; p. 24 t.: laif/Dieter Klein; p. 24/25: Mauritius; p. 25 r.: M/imagebroker; p. 26 t. l.: Arco/R. Hicker; p. 26 t. r.: Huber/ G. Simeone; p. 26/27: Visum/Rolf Nobel; p. 27: Arco/R. Hicker; p. 28 t.: alimdi/Lubenow; p. 28/29: Corbis/Andria Patino; p. 29: Premium/Alessandro Villa; p. 30 t. l.: Huber/Fantuz Olimpio; p. 30 t. r.: Huber/Cogoli Franco; p. 30/31: Huber/p. Scattolin; p. 32 l.: Ifa/Stadler; p. 32 t. l.: Huber/Brozzi Stefano; p. 32 t. r.: Brigitte Gronau, Weilheim; p. 32/33: Corbis/ Pelletier; p. 33 r.: Brigitte Gronau, Weilheim; p. 34 t. l.: laif/Contrasto; p. 34/35: laif/Le Figaro Magazine; p. 36 t. l.: laif/Zinn; p. 36/37 and 37: Huber/G. Simeone; p. 38 t.:

Huber/Kaos03; p. 38/39: H. + D. Zielske; p. 40 t.: laif/Dieter Klein; p. 40/41 and 41: akg; p. 42 t.: Bildarchiv Monheim/ Schuetze; p. 42/43: Look/Rainer Martini; p. 43 r.: Getty/Todd Gipstein; p. 44 t. l.: akg; p. 44 t. r.: M/Alamy/Stephan Jesse Taylor; p. 44/45: M/Alamy/Photo 12; p. 45 r.: akg/Touchstone Pictures/Gregory Do; p. 45 b.: Corbis/John Springer Coll.; p. 46 t. and 46/47: M/Alamy/Barry Mason; p. 47 r. m.: M/ Alamy/ Martin Norris; p. 47 t. r.: Look/Sabine Lubenow; p. 47 b. l.: laif/Galli; p. 48 t.: Huber/Graefenhain; p. 48/49: Huber/Lubenow; p. 49 t. r.: Corbis/Stefano Rellandini/Reuters, p. 49 b. r.: picture alliance/dpa; p. 50 t.: Huber; p. 50/51: M/Alamy/Stephan Vowles; p. 51: laif/Keystone/Silvio Fiore; p. 52 t.: M/Alamy/ Reimar Gaertner; p. 52/53: M/Alamy/Nic Cleave Photography; p. 53 r.: Corbis/Atlantide Phototravel; p. 54 t. l.: laif/Sabine Bungert; p. 54 t. r.: Vario Images; p. 54/55, 55 re. (all 3) and 56/57: H. + D. Zielske; p. 60 t.: Corbis/Sergio Pitamitz; p. 60/61: H. + D. Zielske; p. 61: akg/ Gerard Degeorge; p. 62 t.: laif/Gamma; p. 62 b. l.: Huber/ Guido Baviera; p. 62 b. r.: Corbis/ Frederic Soltan; p. 58 t. li.: alimdi.net/ Sabine Lubenow; p. 62/63: Huber/G. Simeone; p. 64: M/imagebroker/ Sabine Lubenow; p. 64/ 65: laif/ Babovic; p. 66 t.: Ruediger Woelk; p. 66/67: H. + D. Zielske; p. 67 r. m.: Mathias Luedecke; p. 67 t. r.: Udo Bernhardt; p. 67 b. r.: Martin Stollwerk/remotephott.com; p. 68 t.: M/Alamy/Lusoltaly; p. 68/ 69: H. + D. Zielske; p. 69 b. l.: akg/Cameraphoto; p. 69 b. r.: Huber/Fischer; p. 70 t. l.: M/Alamy; p. 70 t. r.: laif/Babovic; p. 70/71: laif/Sabine Bungert; p. 71 r. m.: Michael Kneffel; p. 71 t. r.: M/Alamy/Chuck Pefley; p. 71 b. r.: laif/Contrasto; p. 72 t. r.: akg; p. 72/73: artur/Christian Richters; p. 72 r.: Bridgemanart/Alinari; p. 74/75: H. + D. Zielske; p. 78 t.: Huber/Guido Baviera; p. 78/79: laif/ Zanettini; p. 79 r. m.: Huber/ Johanna Huber; p. 79 t. r.: Huber/ Kaos; p. 79 b. r.: Huber/M/Alamy/Rolf Richardson; p. 80 l.: akg/Cameraphoto, p. 80/81: Huber/p. Scattolin; p. 82 t.: Bildagentur-online; p. 82/83: Arco/F. Scholz; p. 83: Eye Ubiquitous Hutchison; p. 84 t.: M/Alamy/Chuck Pefley; p. 84/85: M/ Alamy/Peter Barrit; p. 85: Bridgemanart; p. 86 t.: Corbis/Alinari Archives; p. 86/87: Bridgemanart; p. 87: akg/Erich Lessing; p. 88 t.: Bridgemanart; p. 88/89: Corbis/Atlantide Phototravel; p. 89: dpa/picture-alliance; p. 90 t. r.: akg/Erich Lessing; p. 90/91: Huber/Kaos02; p. 91: M/Alamy/ Worldwide Picture Library; p. 92/ 93: Look/Sabine Lubenow; p. 96 t.: Huber; p. 96/97: Look/Sabine Lubenow; p. 97: laif/The N.Y. Times/Redux; p. 98 t.:

laif/Back; p. 98/99: Huber/Fantuz Olimpio; p. 99 t.: Michael Kneffel; p. 99 m.: M/Alamy; p. 99 b.: laif/Klein; p. 100 t.: Bridgemanart; p. 100 l.: M/Cubo Images; p. 100/101: M/Zinn; p. 101: laif/ REA; p. 102 t.: laif/Celentano; p. 102/103: Schapowalow/Atlantide; p. 103 (all three): Bridgemanart; p. 104 t.: akg/Cameraphoto; p. 104 t. l.: Corbis/ Arte&Immagini; p. 104 b. r.: imagep.de/ AISA; p. 104 t. r.: akg/Cameraphoto; p. 104 b. r. and t. l.: Bridgemanart; p. 105 b. r.: akg; p. 105 r.: Bridgemanart; p. 106 t.: laif/Zanettini; p. 106/107: M/Alamy/David Parker; p. 107 t.: M/Alamy/Loetscher; p. 107 b.: akg/ Erich Lessing; p. 108 t.: laif/Zanettini; p. 108/109: M/inspirestock; p. 109 m.: M/Alamy/Nichols Bird; p. 109 t.: M/Alamy/Stephen Finn; p. 109 b.: bildagentur-online/K. Pritchard; p. 110 t.: M/ Alamy/Jo Chambers; p. 110/111: ifa/ J.Arnold Images; p. 110 b.: akg/ Cameraphoto; p. 112/113: Visum/Alfred Buellesbach; p. 116 t.: Schapowalow/ Atlantide; p. 116 b. l.: Alimdi.net/Sabine Lubenow; p. 116 b. r.: Schapowalow/ Atlantide; p. 116 t. l. Gillan; p. 116/117: Huber; p. 118 t. l.: Corbis/Paul Seheult/ EyeUbiquitous; p.118 t. r.: akg/ Erich Lessing; p. 118/119: Huber/Guido Baviera; p. 119: M/Alamy; p. 120 t.: die Bildstelle/Uwe Gerig, p. 120/121: Bridgemanart; p.121: Bilderberg/Angelika Jakob; p. 122 t.: Huber/Piai Arcangelo; p. 122/123: laif/Celentano; p. 123 m.: Look/ Sabine Lubenow; p. 123 t.: Look/Rainer Martini; p. 123 b.: Look/ Sabine Lubenow; p. 124 t. l.: M/Alamy/Worldwide Picture Library; p. 124 t. r.: M/Alamy/Sarah Quill; p. 124/125: die Bildstelle/Bernd Nasner; p. 125: M/ Alamy/Marc Sadier; p. 126 t. l.: M/Alamy/ Worldwide Picture Library; p. 126 t. r.: Bridgemanart; p. 126/127: Huber/Fantuz Olimpio; p. 127: Huber/Kaos02; p. 128/ 129: H + D Zielske; p. 132 t.: Bridgemanart; p. 132/133: Huber/Guido Baviera; p. 133: M/Alamy/Ross Warner; p. 134 t.: artur/Klaus Frahm; p. 134 l. m.: F1 online/Pallaske; p. 134 t. l.: akg/ Cameraphoto; p. 134 b. r.: Bridgemanart; p. 134 r.: M/Alamy/Sarah Quill; p. 135: laif/Sabine Bungert; p. 136 t.: Alamy/Buttarelli; p. 136/137: M/Alamy/PF Forsberg; p. 137: Bridgemanart; p. 138 t.: Schapowalow/ Atlantide; p. 138/139 and 139: Look/ Sabine Lubenow; p. 140 t.: picture alliance/ akg/cameraphoto; p. 140 l.: Huber/Guido Baviera; p. 140/141: H. + D. Zielske; p. 141 m.: Michael Kneffel; p. 141 t.: imagep.de/ Kelly Han; p. 141 b.: Michael Kneffel; p. 142 t. l.: Getty; p. 142 t. r.: laif/Dario Pignatelli; p. 142/143: Getty, p.143 m.: artur/thomas Spier; p. 143 t.: Getty; p. 143 b.: artur/thomas Spier; p.

144/145: Huber; p. 148 t.: Michael Kneffel; p. 148 b.: M/Cubo Images; p. 148/149: laif/Celentano; p. 149 t.: M/Alamy/DGB; p. 149 b.: M/Alamy/ Tiberius Photography; p. 150 t. l.: laif/Le Figaro Magazine; p. 150 t. r.: laif/VU; p. 150/151 and 151: M/Cubo Images; p. 152 t.: laif/Reporters; p. 152/153: Huber/Fantuz Olimpio; p. 153 m.: M/Alamy/Roberto Soncin Gerometta; p. 153 t.: laif/REA; p. 153 b.: laif/Zauritz; p. 154 t.: Huber/Fantuz Olimpio; p. 154/155: M/Sabine Lubenow; p. 155: Huber/ Johanna Huber; p. 156 t.: M/Alamy/ DYANA; p. 156/157: Huber/ Siering; p. 158 t.: laif/hub; p. 158/159: M/Alamy/Paolo Gallo; p. 159 t. and b.: laif/Le Figaro Magazine; p. 160 t.: Huber/Bernhart; p. 160/161 and 161: Huber/Fantuz Olimpio; p. 162/163: Bilderberg/Ernsting; p. 164 1: Huber/Monheim; p. 164 2: Huber/ Baviera; p. 164 3: A/Worldwide Picture Library; p. 164 4: laif/Galli; p. 165: Hotel Gritti Palace; p. 166 1: Zielske; p. 166 2: alimdi/Lubenow; p. 166 3: M/Alamy/ Farsberg; p. 166 4: Bridgemanart; p. 167: CLP Fotoservice; p. 168 1: laif/Klein; p. 168 2: akg; p. 168 3: Hotel Santa Chiara; p. 168 4: M/Alamy; p. 169: Hotel Santa Chiara; p. 170 1: Huber/Huber; p. 170 2: laif/ Celentano; p. 170 3: Schapo/sime; p. 170 4: M/Alamy; p. 171: Fototeca Enit; p. 172 1: laif/Celentano; p. 172 2: akg; p. 172 3: Fototeca Enit; p. 172 4: laif/Klein; p. 173: CLP Fotoservice; p. 174 1: Zielske; p. 174 2: Huber/Huber; p. 174 3: M/Alamy; p. 174 4: Kelly Han; p. 175 5: Hostaria da Franz; p. 176 1: Huber/Rinaldi; p. 176 2: M/ Alamy; p. 176 3: Huber; p. 176 4: f1online; p. 177: Fototeca Enit; p. 178/179: Ruediger Woelk; p. 180 (all 4): akg; p. 181 t.: Schapo/Atlantide; p. 181 t. bis 183 b.: akg; p. 184 t.: Alamy/World Travel Library; p. 184 l. and b. r.: akg; p. 185 t.: Alamy/Hackenberg; p. 185 l., t. r. and b. r.: akg; p. 186 IPN/Pefley; p. 186 l.: akg; p. 186 r.: akg; p. 187 t.: Schapo/Atlantide; p. 187 t. r. and 187 b. r.: akg; p. 188/189 and 190 1: Premium; p. 190 2: Caffè Quadri; p. 190 3: Al Covo; p. 192 1: M/JIRI; p. 192 2: akg; p. 192 3: Fototeca Enit/Vito Arcomano; p. 194 1: Alamy/Gaertner; p. 194 2: akg; p. 194 3: Bildstelle/Gehrig; p. 194 4: algiubagio; p. 196 1: Matthias Graben; p. 196 2: Huber/Huber; d. 196 3: Fototeca Enit/Vito Arcomano; p. 198 1: Kneffel; p. 198 2: bridgeman; p. 198 3: CLP Fotoservice.

© for the images on pp. 186 b., 187 t. r. and p. 142: VG Bild-Kunst, Bonn.
© for the images on p. 142: Courtesy Galerie Lelong, New York and Studio Stefania Miscetti, Rome.

MONACO BOOKS is an imprint of Verlag Wolfgang Kunth

© Verlag Wolfgang Kunth GmbH & Co.KG, Munich, 2009
Concept: Wolfgang Kunth
Editing and design: Verlag Wolfgang Kunth gmbH&Co.KG
English edition: JMS Books LLP (translation: Malcolm Garrard; editor: Jo Murray, design: co.design)

For distribution please contact:
Monaco Books
C/o Verlag Wolfgang Kunth, Königinstraße 11
80539 München, Germany
Tel: +49 / 89/45 80 20 23
Fax: +49 /89/45 80 20 21
info@kunth-verlag.de

www.monacobooks.com
www.kunth-verlag.de

ISBN 978-3-89944-531-2

Printed in Slovakia

All facts have been researched with the greatest possible care to the best of our knowledge and belief. However, the editors and publishers can accept no responsibility for any inaccuracies or incompleteness of the details provided. The publishers are pleased to receive any information or suggestions for improvement.

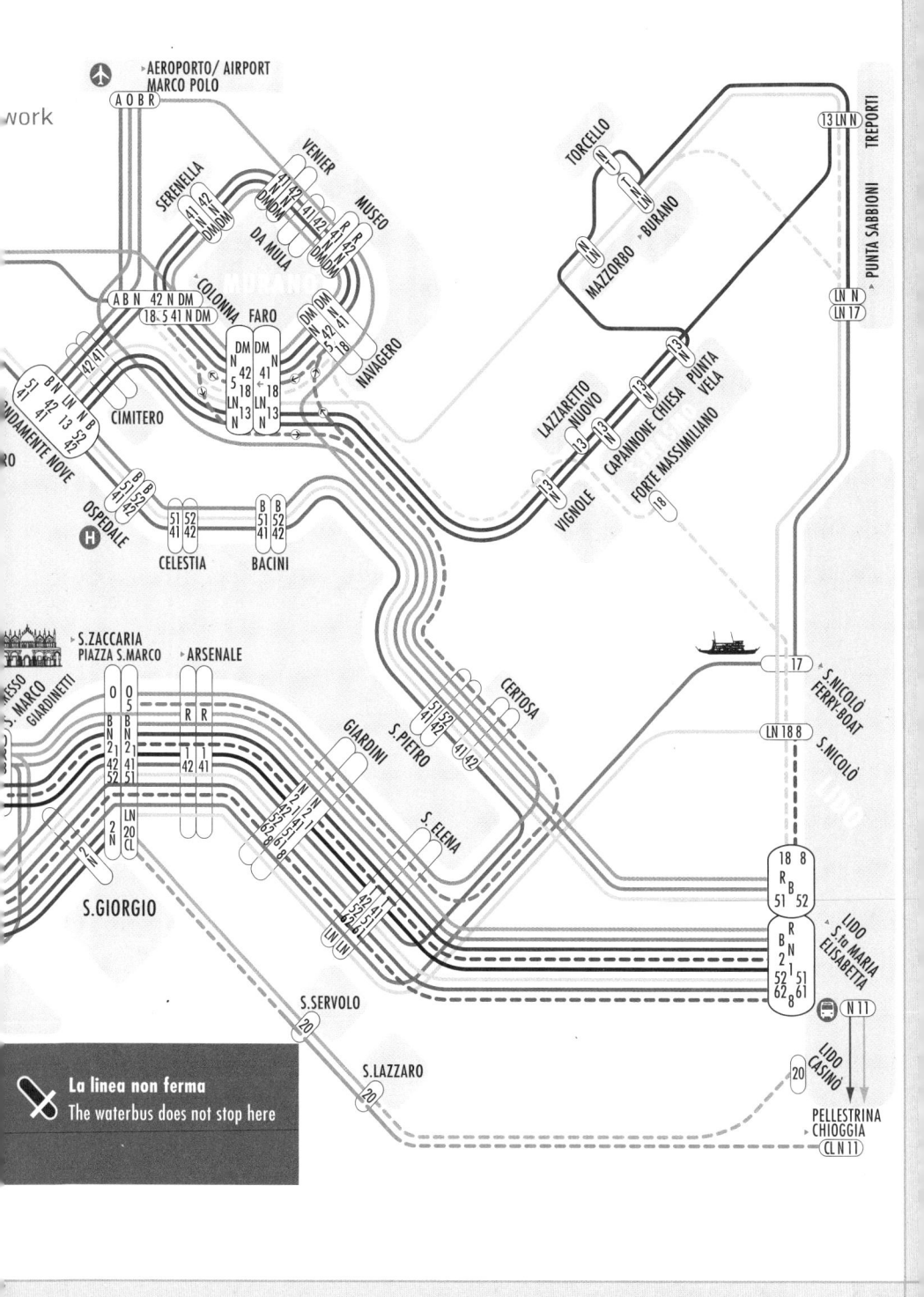